Your Towns and Citi

Norwich
in the Great War

DEDICATION

To all the citizens of the Fine City
who went to fight in the Great War and never came home.

Your Towns and Cities in the Great War

Norwich
in the Great War

Stephen Browning

Pen & Sword
MILITARY

First published in Great Britain in 2015 by
PEN & SWORD MILITARY
an imprint of
Pen and Sword Books Ltd
47 Church Street
Barnsley
South Yorkshire S70 2AS

ISBN 978 1 47382 818 6

A CIP record for this book is available from the British Library.

Printed and bound in England
by CPI Group (UK) Ltd, Croydon, CR0 4YY

Typeset in Times New Roman by Chic Graphics

Pen & Sword Books Ltd incorporates the imprints of
Pen & Sword Archaeology, Atlas, Aviation, Battleground, Discovery,
Family History, History, Maritime, Military, Naval, Politics, Railways,
Select, Social History, Transport, True Crime, Claymore Press,
Frontline Books, Leo Cooper, Praetorian Press, Remember When,
Seaforth Publishing and Wharncliffe.

For a complete list of Pen and Sword titles please contact
Pen and Sword Books Limited
47 Church Street, Barnsley, South Yorkshire, S70 2AS, England
E-mail: enquiries@pen-and-sword.co.uk
Website: www.pen-and-sword.co.uk

Contents

Acknowledgements

Grateful thanks are due to very many people involved in the production of this book.

It would not have been possible without the help, always cheerfully given, by the staff of all the excellent Norfolk libraries and resource centres. Original news material from the period has been extensively preserved and thanks are due to the custodians of this priceless archive.

At Pen & Sword Books I give special thanks to Roni Wilkinson for all his encouragement and help, to Pamela Covey for superb copy-editing, and to Matt Jones for overseeing production.

Finally, thank you to my friends – you know who you are – who have read various sections and made useful suggestions.

Introduction

On the eve of the Great War, Norwich was very much a city on the rise: an industrial and commercial powerhouse. It was most certainly also not without its problems, notably the extreme poverty of some areas such as the notorious Norwich Yards. Both of these factors impacted on the war and subsequent changes to the city.

This book looks at Norwich and the surrounding areas on the eve of conflict and charts everyday life in the city year on year, extensively using original material from the period. It very much focuses on how it felt to live in the city, on the joy and sadness, on the changes to people's lives, on the courage and humour, as well as the pride and determination shown by the people of 'The Fine City'. Both dramatic events and the details of daily life are illustrated by many unique photographs taken at the time.

Norwich industry made a vital contribution to the war effort in ways both big and small, from making pairs of boots in their hundreds of thousands and the Sopwith Camel aircraft to literally smaller things that had an appreciable psychological impact, such as Caley's Marching Chocolate for the troops, and the patriotic books and gifts made by Jarrolds in previously unprecedented quantities. All these are celebrated here.

Most importantly, this account details the incredible deeds of the heroes who travelled from Norwich to the fields of conflict, some of whom gained the Victoria Cross but many more who did not. An 'At a Glance' section per year gives the main world events during which these actions took place and against which home life unfolded. It concludes with a view of the city as the surviving troops finally came home.

A closing appendix gives the route for a fascinating 'Great War Walk' around the city centre, taking in many of the places discussed in this book.

CHAPTER 1

Norwich, 'The Fine City', on the Eve of the Great War

Never yet did a stranger visit Norwich and wander with an intelligent eye through its sinuous streets without experiencing that indescribable charm and delight consequent upon the succession of picturesque prospects which burst upon the view in the numerous combinations of medieval ecclesiastical architecture with the bustle and stir of mercantile establishments.
Citizens of No Mean City, Jarrold and Sons, Norwich, April 1910

The term 'A Fine City' is taken from the novel *Lavengro* by celebrated Norwich writer George Borrow, published in 1851. What he actually wrote was 'a fine old city, truly is that...' but the word 'old' was later omitted. It has now become the city's slogan. It did not catch on straight away, however, and on the eve of the Great War many referred to Norwich as 'No Mean City' which is taken from St Paul's description of Tarsus, a town in Cilicia.

Industrial and commercial might
The city was an Edwardian industrial powerhouse with some of its firms destined to play a vital role in the war. These included Boulton

& Paul, already producing virtually anything in metal from wire netting to aircraft bodies; Colman's, who cut down on the acreage given over to mustard production for the duration of hostilities in order to grow more essential crops and were to see 921 men join up, including four of the seven directors; Howlett and White, and

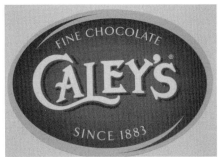

many other shoe producers, who together made literally millions of pairs of what was universally agreed to be the perfect marching boot for the British and allied armies; and Caley's who produced chocolate bars that were sent to hundreds of thousands of troops on the front lines. 'Caley's Marching Chocolate' was especially popular and can still be bought in Caley's Coffee Shop in the Old Guildhall on the Market Place.

The schoolroom at Colman's Carrow Works. Colman's provided education for the children of the workers; also a health scheme, hot meals, a social club and even housing in a purpose-built village.

Beer

Norwich had also been famous since Victorian times for beer production with at least seven large breweries such as Youngs, Crawshay and Youngs, and Bullard's, along with dozens of malt houses. This was very much a mixed blessing as it is estimated that the city had over 500 public houses, many of which were unlicensed, being nothing more than the front rooms of wretched houses in areas of the city such as Coslany where poverty was rife. City magistrates continually ordered such establishments, which found it easy to buy a barrel of ale from a brewery literally 'up the road' and sell it in an attempt to eke out a living, to be closed down only for another to open up, often next door or nearby.

It was felt morally necessary to offer help against the demon drink

Bullard's Brewery is now residential accommodation.

which was a significant problem and was one factor in the often poor physical condition of those offering themselves for recruitment to the army. The Independent Order of Rechabites, Temperance Friendly Society, announced that it 'admits Males and Females, Adults and Juveniles, to Membership' and had the slogan 'We Live in Deeds Not Words'. The United Kingdom Provident Institution claimed to be 'The Best Office for Abstainers'. Drunkenness was a continual theme in the local courts of Norwich.

Banking, insurance and shops

The city was also a main Empire centre for the banking and insurance industries. The famous Norwich Union Mutual Insurance Company, now renamed Aviva, had its exquisite headquarters in Surrey Street built by George Skipper from imported Italian marble in 1903/04 (it is magnificent and still fully open to view by the public today). Total funds in 1908 amounted to £8,823,303. Gurney's Bank, now part of Barclays, created the phrase common at the time 'as rich as the Gurneys'. Farrows Bank Ltd operated from the Market Place and advertisements in the local press read: 'It Caters for All Classes, It Offers Sound Security'.

There were some fine stores too. One, still very much thriving today, was Jarrold and Sons. In Edwardian times it advertised itself in various ways, including as 'a travelling goods specialist', 'The Noted Book Shop' and 'The Noted Gift House', all of which it still is, but before the Great War it also boasted 'Jarrolds Select Library – Free Use to an Entire Family of a well-appointed Reading Room; subscriptions from 10/6 per Annum'. Other stores included Tuxford Trunks which asked 'Are your trunks all right? Tuxford Trunks are Porter-proof. No 3 Back-of-the-Inns, Norwich'. Messrs Arthur Bunting and Co. Ltd of St Stephen's Corner and Rampant Horse Street described itself as being 'Quite in the front rank of the leading Drapery and Furnishing Houses of Norwich'. Many were quick to adapt to change. As flying in aircraft became the latest very exciting – often fatal in those early days – activity for the daring, the *Eastern Daily Press* reported that confectioners Snelling's of Rampant Horse Street, Norwich had a new delicacy on offer: aviation cakes. 'Very light and easily digestible', they were on sale for one shilling in a choice of nine flavours: almond, cherry, walnut, rose, orange, lemon, violet, chocolate and coffee.

London Street in 1905 and today.

Wages, jobs, goods, prices and entertainment

Wages for an agricultural worker were about £75 a year. There was a great demand for servants. The *Eastern Daily Press* daily carried advertisements for cook-housekeepers at annual wages of £75, £65 or £45, dependent on experience. Another agency, advertising in the *Norwich Mercury*, called for nurses, housemaids, parlour-maids, cooks, second housemaids, under-housemaids, cooks-general, kitchen-maids, scullery-maids and between-maids at yearly salaries of £10 to £30. Applicants were to call in person at 78 Prince of Wales Road (still an office today). The *Norfolk Chronicle* was advertising, at the turn of the year, for Royal Navy Boys aged 15 to 18 who were to report just down by the station at 54 Riverside Road. Lads were also wanted as farmworkers in Australia, for which the fare was £3.

There were all sorts of medicines and ointments for sale for which claims were made that would not be permitted today. The *Norfolk Chronicle* promoted Syrup of Camphor as a 'Great Lung Healer – eases coughs, wards off consumption'. Another advertisement claimed 'Luxuriant Hair, long flowing eye lashes are quickly produced using James' Herbal Pomade', while the makers of Lockyer's Sulphur Hair

George Skipper's Royal Arcade c. 1906.

George Skipper's Royal Arcade today.

Restorer gave this advice: 'Don't look old! Keep your Employment'. The Victoria Garage, Norwich was advertising a Torpedo Phantom motor car for £500. The Cromer Theatre of Varieties was publicizing a new production '*I Shall Avenge* – a thrilling drama', while Yarmouth Hippodrome was competing with an 'Aquatic Review: *Hoist Yer Slacks*'.

At the time, milk cost 2d (old pennies) a pint, 1lb of bacon was a shilling and a loaf of bread just over 5d. Loans were available by post: '£10–£1000'. 'Gentleman's Lounge suits, perfectly tailored,' were offered in the *Norwich Mercury* at 32/6.

Trams and inventions

Norwich engineers were the proud builders of a fine city-wide tram network, operational from 1901, although how to illuminate the cars while not showing a light to the enemy was to prove problematic during the first years of the war. Another achievement that was to cause even greater difficulty with regard to making the city invisible to passing Zeppelins was the project, headed by city electrical engineer F.M. Long, which installed 1,750 electric lights in the streets between 1911 and 1913.

Norwich has always managed to produce men of invention and

Proud Norwich citizens pose on one of their brand-new trams, c. 1902.

Guildhall Hill today.

vision in all manner of fields, from banking and insurance to mustard, chocolate, anaesthetics and ballooning. One whose ideas did not materialize but might have had a dramatic impact on the war was a Mr W.J. Botterill who, in 1909, proposed a new plan for Norfolk to be the premier naval base for Great Britain, which at the time was Rosyth in Scotland. He proposed a canal from the River Yare at Berney Arms to Norwich with a massive naval base 4 miles outside Norwich at Rockland Broad. Finally, he suggested a 240-mile ship canal across England from the North Sea to the Bristol Channel. Quite a few major cities would thus become docks with links to the sea, including Cambridge, Bedford and Oxford. Finances permitting, a further channel could be dug linking Oxford and Birmingham. Alas, this never came to be as the cost would have been too great and this was at a time when many were pointing out the antiquity of some ships in the navy and the need for their replacement.

Partying to conflict

In the nation as a whole, the Edwardian period – roughly from 1901 to the outbreak of war – is often seen as a 'golden time': of regattas on the Thames, of horse-racing, of rich and opulent fashions and, politically, of great world power. One man who exemplified this was the new king, Edward VII. Following the restraint of the old queen's declining years, the nation wanted a party and the king was more than happy to lead it. In reality, England's dominance was already beginning its decline and many historians trace the break-up of Empire directly to this period. Both America and Germany were overtaking England in the efficiency of manufacturing processes and, as the sinking of three British cruisers – the *Hogue, Aboukir* and *Cressy* – in 1914 by one German U-boat within the space of ninety minutes made plain to a shocked public, British naval dominance was by no means a given any longer.

Royal recognition and political change

Norwich itself was changing, too. The importance of the city was recognized when on 25 October 1909 King Edward VII became the first monarch to visit Norwich since Charles II, 238 years previously. From 1910 the mayor became a lord mayor; one of only fifteen cities in the kingdom to be granted this distinction. George V was to visit the city on 28 June 1911, a mere six days after his coronation. Norwich undoubtedly had growing clout.

Politically, this was a transformative time for women's rights. From 1907 women could stand for the city council, the first elected being Mabel Clarkson in 1913. Emmeline Pankhurst spoke above male catcalls at St Andrew's Hall in December 1912 (apparently the main chant to drown her out was 'On the Ball, City' which today can be

Suffragettes in Prince of Wales Road, Norwich in 1914.

heard all over the southern slopes of Norwich whenever the 'Canaries' are playing at home). Just after the war, Norwich became the first city in the country to have a female lord mayor, Ethel Colman, daughter of Jeremiah James Colman; her sister, Helen, acted as lady mayoress.

A beautiful city with lots of apples

Citizens of No Mean City, published by Jarrold and Sons – as well as owning Norwich's premier department store and private library, the Jarrold family also operated a printing works – had this to say in 1910: 'Few cities are more beautifully situated than Norwich, through which winds the meandering Wensum, while the waterways on every hand, penetrating or bounding its pleasant suburbs, almost enclose as in a silvery cincture, the capital of the county of the Broads.' Looking at artwork and old photographs of the period it does, indeed, appear beautiful in a more rural sense than we know it today and in one respect in particular this was to have a direct bearing on the feeding of the

St George's Colegate in the early twentieth century.

troops. In Tudor times, Norwich had been described as 'a city in an orchard or an orchard in a city', so great were the number and variety of apple trees to be seen. In the first part of the century the apple crop was still of great importance and apples – often with plums – were a staple of soldiers on the front line. Indeed, so plentiful were the supplies that rations containing apples were the butt of many military jokes and great was the joy and hilarity when an apple-free meal was produced. It is practically impossible to see an apple tree in central Norwich today and many varieties have been lost. We can only wonder at the magic of some of the names: Norwich Jubilee; Caroline, from Blickling, named after Lord Suffield's wife; Norfolk Nonpareil; Royal Coast Russet; St Magdalen; and Colonel Harbord's Pippin.

The floods of 1912

Norwich was in the news for an altogether different reason in 1912: flooding caused by excessive rain. On 27 August the city's lights went out as the electric power station failed under 6ft of water. Over 3,500

Cheerful cleaning-up in Magdalen Street after the floods of 1912.

The first ever flight in Norfolk on 3 August 1912. Mr B.C. Hucks is flying his monoplane 'Firefly'.

houses were affected, many in the poverty-stricken Yards running down to the river in the north of the city. These were the people previously referred to who tried everything, including selling beer from their front rooms, to make ends meet. They had no voice and had been largely ignored for a long time, except when they appeared in court, which was every week, most often for drunkenness, immoral behaviour, swearing and stealing. Now, however, the national press took up their case; not entirely out of the goodness of their hearts but because there was a growing fear that war may be coming and people from these backgrounds would be needed in the armed forces. On the positive side, there were many tales of friendship and heroism as people sailed up the streets in whatever boats they could find, distributing food and warm drinks. Local shops and manufacturers such as Caley's provided drinks of chocolate and milk in bottles that had a loop of string on the neck and were passed to upper windows on a pole with a hook on the end.

A sense of pride

Thus all was not well in this period; certainly Norwich was not enjoying a magical Edwardian summer any more than the rest of the country. However, if you had a job and a decent home, life could seem rosy. Even if you did not, there was a feeling that life could change; education and, increasingly, votes were for everyone, and there were many wonders to engage the mind. The overall feeling was a positive one of pride, both in the country and the city, exemplified by a contemporary local writer: 'A great wave of industrial prosperity was passing over the country, and Norfolk, especially its capital, was more or less directly feeling its stimulus. Employment was brisk, money was circulating freely, an air of general well-being existed.'

Norwich was famous for shoe production: the inside of a typical finishing room.

CHAPTER 2

1914:
Eager for a Fight

1914 at a glance
• 28 June: Serbian Nationalists shoot dead Archduke Ferdinand, heir to the throne of the Austro-Hungarian Empire, and his wife Sophie.
• 23 July: Austria-Hungary issues a reply in the form of an ultimatum and gives Serbia forty-eight hours to respond.
• 24 July: Germany announces support for Austria.
• 25 July: Russia sends troops to the Austrian frontier and Serbia mobilizes.
• 28 July: Austria-Hungary declares war on Serbia.
• 31 July: General mobilization begins in Russia and Austria. Germany demands that Russian military preparations are halted within twelve hours. Britain asks France and Germany to declare their support for Belgian neutrality; only France responds.
• 1 August: Germany declares war on Russia. France mobilizes.
• 3 August: Germany declares war on France. Britain mobilizes. Germany demands passage across Belgium for its troops. Britain issues ultimatum to Austria-Hungary to stand down from fighting.
• 4 August: No guarantee received from Germany. Britain declares war on Germany.
• 20 August: Brussels is occupied by Germany; this is where Nurse Edith Cavell is working.
• 24 August: 1st Norfolks involved in retreat from Mons, their first action of the war.

• 31 August: Public meeting at St Andrew's Hall, Norwich leads to 'recruitment surge'.
• 6 September: First Battle of the Marne. German advance checked.
• 22 September: German submarine *U-9* sinks three old British cruisers – *Hogue*, *Aboukir* and *Cressy* – in ninety minutes; many Norfolk reservists are killed.
• 19 October: First Battle of Ypres.
• 3 November: Great Yarmouth and Gorleston bombarded by German ships.
• 22 November: Trench warfare begins in earnest on the Western Front.
• 25 December: Christmas Day and many informal truces are temporarily declared along the Western Front; gifts are exchanged and an impromptu football match is played.

The coming of war
'One day the great European War will come out of some damned foolish thing in the Balkans' (Otto von Bismarck, 1888).

Assassination of Archduke Franz Ferdinand and the Duchess of Hohenberg
On Sunday, 28 June 1914 the Archduke Franz Ferdinand and his wife Sophie, Duchess of Hohenberg, were assassinated in Sarajevo, the capital of Bosnia, as they were driving away from the Town Hall following a reception. Gavrilo Princip was the assassin. The bomb that had been thrown was reported to be a 'bottle bomb' filled with lead and iron filings and it injured twenty other people around the royal couple.

Will war come to Norfolk?
The summer of 1914 was hot and in Norfolk as elsewhere, those who could had decamped to the coast. The fears brought about by the assassination of Franz Ferdinand and his wife Sophie were surely exaggerated. No one, people believed, would risk destabilizing the world order and taking on the might of the British Empire. At worst, the overwhelming feeling was that the conflict would be contained.

However, on 23 July, nearly a month after the tragedy, the Austro-Hungarian government presented a note to Serbia full of strong demands. A reply was requested within forty-eight hours. Serbia asked Russia for guidance and, acting on advice received from this most important Slav power, Serbia replied within the time limit accepting all but two of the Austrian demands. She requested that these two items be referred to The Hague Tribunal. This proved unacceptable and on Saturday, 26 July the Austro-Hungarian Minister left Belgrade, effectively declaring war on Serbia.

Friday 31 July to Tuesday 4 August

'He that all England would win
Should at Weybourne Hope begin.'
(Old Norfolk saying)

The weekend of Friday, 31 July to Tuesday, 4 August was one of extraordinary tension in Norfolk. It had been believed ever since the Spanish Armada that the exceptionally deep seas off Weybourne presented a very likely spot for invasion. Nevertheless, the hope was still that somehow any conflict would be contained. Diplomats may have been making increasingly frenetic efforts to secure peace and, although European armies were mobilizing, a great many Norfolk people were primarily concerned about making their way to the seaside.

Over the weekend, matters changed critically and very fast. On the Saturday Germany declared war on Russia and on Sunday German troops violated the neutrality of Luxembourg. To the demands from Germany that Belgium should allow free passage of her troops, the small nation refused and asked England for assistance. The British government asked Germany for an assurance that the neutrality of Belgium would be respected. On Tuesday, 4 August Sir Edward Grey requested a reply from Germany before midnight.

In response to concerns that expenditure on the navy was inadequate, the Navy League declared on 31 July that 'it is in the position to declare with a full knowledge of the facts... that the condition of the British Fleet is, at the present moment, equal to any emergency.'

It was far from universally agreed that Great Britain should become involved at all. On 3 August the *Eastern Daily Press* had this to say:

Hopefully war will be avoided and if the British people must unhappily be involved in the madness of Europe it will, we are sure, be in despite of the steady desire of the whole nation for peace and for a very much deeper reason than the mere desire to smash up the German fleet, which is plainly the principal object of the new jingoes.

On the same day there was a demonstration in Norwich against the war. On 4 August the *Eastern Daily Press* asked: 'What is England to do?' and carried a piece by Baron von Kühlmann of the German Embassy in London entitled: 'Why Britain should be neutral'. Of one thing the paper was certain, though: the need to keep calm. 'Do not hoard food,' it wrote. 'That sort of panicky action is foolish and useless.'

Nonetheless, the majority view was undoubtedly that war should not be avoided or the enemy appeased. It would be short, even fun – very soon posters were to appear on Norwich streets calling on men to 'Come and Join Our Happy Band' – and a chance to give the Germans a bloody nose. On 5 August almost 300 men attached to the Norwich Division of the National Reserves paraded at the Agricultural Hall.

In court
Meanwhile, normal city life continued. The court based at the Guildhall – now a café that still retains the magistrates' elevated seating – was busy as usual. On 5 and 8 August the *Eastern Daily Press* reported the following cases:

• Alfred Harvey, a labourer, was charged with being drunk in charge of a child aged 5 in St Stephens Street. He was further charged with assaulting Police Constable Albert Robinson in the Market Place on the same day. Prisoner said he was very sorry. He had been in Navy and gone round the globe, and had met up with some old mates. Fined 5s.
• George White, 64, found drunk and incapable in London Street. Fined 2s.
• Alice White, found guilty of using indecent language in St Swithin's Alley. Fined 5s.
• William Lovett, 12, charged with using obscene language at Cattle Market. Fined 2s.
• Edward Smith, 45, labourer, was charged with being drunk whilst in charge of a horse and cart at St Benedict's Street. Fined 10s with 5s 6d costs.

• Joseph Somerville, Horse Clipper, was charged with using threats against a woman in Norwich on 27 June. Complainant, a single woman, said prisoner had lodged with her close upon 3 years. About four o'clock in the afternoon she asked the lodger to leave the house whereupon he said he would not go for anybody and threatened to 'push her face in'. She no longer felt safe in her own house and was afraid the prisoner would murder her. Prisoner was bound over to keep the peace and ordered to pay 9s costs.
• Bertie Hagg, 63, pleaded guilty to riding a bicycle without light in Prince of Wales Road. Fined 2s.

Ironically, regarding the last case, just a few months later people would appear before the court for riding WITH lights around the city.

Suffragettes
The outbreak of war had done little to dampen the ardour of the suffragettes. The *Norwich Mercury* ran an article in July that listed their deeds since the beginning of 1913. Within that time they had set fire to 8 churches; exploded bombs in 6 churches; set fire to 36 houses; fired 22 cricket pavilions or other buildings of that type; tried to burn down 19 schools, railway stations and timber yards; and made 24 attempts to damage pictures in public galleries. None of this takes into account all the failed attempts in each category which are similar in number to those that actually occurred. The total cost of just the damage that had been insured against was estimated to be £384,000.

On 6 August trading was stopped at Norwich Corn Market because, according to the local press, 'farmers were unwilling to sell on account of the uncertainty of national events'. The *Eastern Daily Press* wrote: 'We have no doubt that the mood of Norwich was the mood everywhere, a mood of grim quietness more terrible than any shouting and flag-waving could be.' It reported that the financial markets were 'distressful'. The *Norwich Mercury* said that, in common with other newspapers, it had decided '…. in view of the existing circumstances of national concern, not to publish for the present any news concerning the movement of British troops'.

The gravity of the situation was sinking in and the public was keen to help. On 8 August the *Norwich Evening News* carried a letter from Alice Orde:

Sirs, As hospitals will be anxious to get rid of their ordinary cases as soon as possible in order to take in naval and military patients, would it not be a good plan if everyone with a spare room should place it at the disposition of the nearest hospital and be prepared to take in one or two convalescents?

Lord Kitchener's appeal for 100,000 men was launched. The same newspaper carried, on 18 August, a report of the 'veritable butchery' of Belgians by Germans at Louvain. It was proposed, once again in the letters page, that Germans in the country should be rounded up and sent to a colony. Another letter suggested the banning of German sausage dogs. On 24 August Germans were required to begin registration and this proceeded without incident, the *Evening News* reporting: 'The registration of aliens has gone on pleasantly enough in Norwich. It has not been marked by any protests or incidents as has been the case elsewhere.'

First call-up

The first men to receive instructions regarding the dire state of events were those of the Naval Reserve, most of whom lived on the coast or in the villages just inland. It was just before dawn on the Sunday morning that the Admiralty issued an order calling up all classes of naval reserves. Motor cars and bicycles rushed to inform nearby villages of the news and a cutter was dispatched into the Wash with instructions for the fishing fleet. In King's Lynn forty-eight out of the sixty Naval Reservists had presented themselves at the Customs House by one o'clock the following day and they left by train for Chatham, cheered by enthusiastic crowds, the same afternoon.

The atmosphere on Bank Holiday Monday, 3 August when the seaside resorts of Norfolk were crowded was one of optimism but determination that, if things did not change, then so be it. This is how the *Peace Souvenir*, published by the famous Norwich printing and retail firm of Jarrold and Sons in 1919, recalled the mood:

Beneath the surface jollity of the day there brooded a spirit of disquietude, which deepened as the hours passed and no reply was received from Germany to the English request. Never was war less desired by any nation than by the English people at this

Edwardians paddling in the sea at Great Yarmouth.

time. But never was a nation more united in its determination not to stoop to any dishonourable peace. Not in excited demonstrations, but in a collective demeanour neither expressive of fear nor of callous disregard of consequences, did the national temper find outward expression.

War is declared
At the time, the *Eastern Daily Press* had offices at Norwich, Yarmouth, Cromer and Lowestoft, and it was here that people gathered to read the latest bulletins. This firm then also published a sister newspaper, the *Eastern Evening News,* and it was here, when a fresh edition was issued

just before midnight on the hot night of Tuesday, 4 August that people read the following:

> Owing to the summary rejection by the German Government of the request made by His Majesty's Government for assurances that the neutrality of Belgium will be respected, His Majesty's Ambassador in Berlin has received his passports, and His Majesty's Government have declared to the German Government that a state of war exists between Great Britain and Germany as from eleven p.m. on August 4th.

The Norfolk coast prepares

It was on the Norfolk coast that defensive measures were first introduced. Settlements such as Happisburgh and Weybourne were considered prime sites for a hostile landing as the sea there was deep enough to allow ships to closely approach the shoreline and land men and machines. Immediate action was taken to defend them. In Happisburgh, for example, a division of what were known as 'Rough Riders' – cavalry hastily drafted in from all over the country – were billeted in private houses. Trenches were dug along the clifftops and the beaches closed to the public completely between sunset and sunrise; at all other times special permission needed to be obtained from the lieutenant colonel in charge of defences. In addition, many local women were organized into groups to make clothing and bandages for the troops.

On 8 August the herring fleet was ordered back to port and all fishing was suspended. The *Norwich Mercury* reported: 'The great fleets of Europe and millions of armed men are making feverish preparations for a conflict which dwarfs into absolute insignificance any previous struggle in the history of the world.' It then added: '... who will be the victor in this Titanic struggle, no man can foresee....' On the same day came reports of the capture of the first German prisoners, as well as the seizure of the steamer *Belgia* at Newport with a number of German reservists and large quantity of food, and news of the first German naval loss of the war, the auxiliary minelayer *Königin Luise* of 2,150 tons, which had been sunk on 5 August.

On 15 August the grounds and gardens of Sandringham were closed to visitors. On the same day, German spies were reported to be using racing pigeons to carry messages to Germany. On 28 August German floating mines were reported off The Wash.

Norwich

Meanwhile, in Norwich the authorities had no previous experience to rely on when deciding what to do in the event of an invasion. It was decided that Local Emergency Committees should be formed under the direction of the Lord Lieutenant, the Earl of Leicester. A Central Organizing Committee for Norfolk was formed of which the representatives for Norwich were the Lord Mayor, Mr J.A. Porter and the Town Clerk, Mr Arnold J. Miller. Thereafter, Local Emergency Committees were set up throughout the county. In Norwich the Lord Mayor, Sheriff, Deputy Mayor, City Engineer and Chief Constable volunteered for the Local Emergency Committee. The Norwich Committee consulted with the government regarding the best ways of helping the armed forces and of repelling and hampering any invasion.

The first arrangements to be made concerned motor vehicles and garages. Lists of all motor vehicles and motor-cycles were prepared. The new Lord Mayor, Dr J.G. Gordon-Munn, asked the public to register their vehicles for military use if necessary: 200 motor cars and a similar number of motor-cycles were listed. While 300 drivers volunteered to serve, instructions were issued to people who did NOT offer their vehicles for military use for their disablement to prevent them falling into enemy hands. Some 100 mechanics capable of disabling motor engines were sworn in as special constables. Garages, stockists of tyres, petrol and engine parts were issued with specific instructions as to amounts and storage methods of such items, as well as how to move or destroy them if so ordered.

Another order established the Civilian Emergency Corps, originally of 1,200 people, one purpose of which was to remove or destroy horses if necessary. (In total, millions of horses and other animals were put to military use during the Great War and it was essential that those not 'conscripted' for allied service should not be available to the enemy.) In addition, foodstuffs, cattle, boats and any other items of possible use to the enemy were to be destroyed upon the instructions of special constables.

Next, the Norwich Division of the British Medical Association was set up to deal with civilian casualties. Schools were appointed as dressing stations and specific doctors were to report to each of these if enemy aircraft were spotted.

In case of an influx of refugees – it was believed that there could be as many as 50,000 – cocoa was to be stockpiled. Public buildings would be used to house these people.

In the worst-case scenario where an invasion could not be effectively halted, people were to retreat inland and orders would be issued nearer the time giving directions. In the meantime, Boy Scouts were organized to check out the lie of the land and find alternatives to the main roads in the event of this becoming necessary.

At the end of August the Reverend F.J. Meyrick, vicar of St Peter Mancroft, said that it was no claptrap or cant to say that this was a religious war. 'Never has a nation,' he said, 'had a more righteous cause.'

The War Relief Executive Committee helped the wives and families of serving soldiers. On 25 August 1914 the Lord Mayor Mr J.A. Porter became President of the Soldiers' and Sailors' Families Association which was then responsible for administering grants from the National Relief Fund for the widows of servicemen. Many volunteers also helped.

Women make sandbags at Carrow Road.

Home defence

In November 1914 the *Eastern Daily Press* began to advertise for older men – those over 38 years of age – to create a Volunteer Training Corps that was officially formed on 4 December in the Agricultural Hall under the command of Lieutenant Colonel Leathes Prior. They held their first parade on 15 December and a year later there were twenty-eight squads drilling in various public buildings three times a week. On Thursdays and Saturdays they drilled on the Earlham Recreation Ground. Such men came from all professions. The authorities seemed ambivalent, even unsupportive, at first and the public named them 'England's Last Hope' and 'the Cripples Brigade'. Indeed, parades sometimes had a comic aspect with elderly men bumping into each other and some unable to distinguish left from right.

As the war progressed, the quality of volunteer units declined. One, the 49th Provisional Battalion, was dubbed 'the Grocers' and consisted of soldiers who had returned wounded from the front line and men considerably over age, some quite infirm. These men were usually sent to the coast to guard against invasion.

Rural communities

The rural communities just outside Norwich also played their part. Lingwood, Beighton and Burlingham, about 10 miles from the city, became a centre for sick and injured horses that had been shipped back from France; up to twenty horses at a time could be catered for.

The Specials

Special Constables were people whose interests or occupation exempted them from purely military service. By becoming 'Specials', they were able to release many from the regular police force to the army.

By 28 August the registration of Special Constables had proceeded over four consecutive days. By that time 170 had registered but an appeal was launched for at least 400; it was pointed out that the more came forward, the shorter would be the turn of duty for each one.

In the early days there was some discontent as they had nothing to do. Another part of the problem was that they did not 'look the part' as cloth for uniforms was scarce. They had to wait until January 1916 for their caps and until August of that year for a blue uniform. Overcoats did not materialize until February 1917. The Chief Constable at the time was Mr E.F. Winch and he organized the men into 4 companies with 4 commanders, 8 sub-commanders and about 60 to 70 sergeants. The Lord Mayor and Sheriff became honorary commanders.

Initially each Special was placed on duty with a regular policeman. Part of their duty was to guard sensitive spots such as bridges and the gas and electricity works. To keep the men fit, route marches were organized on Sundays. One of them was from Norwich to Wroxham and Coltishall and back to Norwich. Relations between the two forces were excellent. The Specials volunteered to take over Christmas duty on Christmas Day 1916 so that the regulars could have a day with their families, and this custom continued for the duration of the war.

Probably the most valuable task was air-raid duty in all weathers. Often a Special would be on air-raid duty having already spent a normal day at work. Many kept awake by drinking copious quantities of coffee.

Some of them formed a corps of motor car and motor-cycle men, trained to carry dispatches and for specific duties in the event of invasion. There were 10 such motor cars, 15 motor-cycles and 25 cycles, each man having to supply his own machine. There was also an ambulance corps. Mr E.J. Caley was responsible for forming a Special Constables' Rifle Corps that practised at a rifle range in his grounds at Thorpe. Initially some objected to practice on a Sunday until told by Mr Caley 'in a time of national emergency it is right and proper that people should not object to learning to defend their homes and families on a Sunday.' The club numbered around 300 members.

Very popular among the Specials was the game of bowls. Commanders such as Mr E.E. Hines put their fine lawns at the disposal of the men. Mr Winsor Bishop, MBE, gave a silver challenge cup for an inter-company tournament. The Lord Mayor presented each of the twelve winning teams with a silver spoon as a souvenir.

Tobacco and smoking

Smoking concerts and whist drives were among many events organized for both social and fund-raising purposes. Smoking cigarettes was seen as promoting camaraderie and important for morale during sometimes long tedious days or convalescence from injury. Local communities vied with each other to send cigarettes and pipe tobacco to the front, and often at home would slip these to passing troops as a sign of support. Mass-marketing campaigns for different brands began and have only ceased in recent times. Tobacco and cigarettes probably only came a very close second to food among the needs of the serving man. British soldiers and sailors smoked 1,000 tons of cigarettes and 700 tons of pipe tobacco in 1915 alone.

Mass cigarette marketing was given a huge boost by the conflict.

The coast takes the brunt of enemy attack

Norwich was fortunate to be situated inland as the coastal communities battled against Zeppelins and German naval attacks. The first confused but spectacular appearance by the enemy was off the coast of Gorleston on 3 November 1914. Crowds lined the cliffs to watch the guns of the three battle-cruisers and three light cruisers. Unfortunately air support was unavailable as any air machines were undergoing repair at the time, and a submarine launched from Yarmouth tragically ran into a mine and was lost. However, there was only one enemy shell that landed and this was a dud.

Recruitment rush and Pals brigades

The war led to a recruitment rush, no doubt helped by women dishing out white feathers to those they considered cowards. Enlistment was not confined to the working class. The 'Pals battalions' contained many men from the middle classes. The sense that Britain was 'all in it together' was heightened when the son of the Irish Earl of Granard was killed at the Battle of Mons on 23 August.

Attleborough is typical of a Norfolk village popular with recruiters; this was because it had a railway station that could immediately whisk young men away to training camps. It was also notable for Pals' recruitment as whole cricket and football teams signed up together. Within a few days of the war 35 had enrolled and by the end 550; this out of a total population of just 2,500. Inevitably, this meant that women had to increasingly take on unfamiliar roles such as in mechanical engineering and on the land.

Another example of mass Pals' signing-up was in the village of

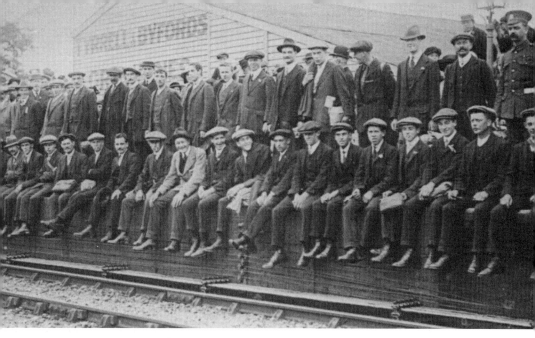

Volunteers waiting for the train at Attleborough Station, Norfolk in August 1914.

Carrow Works clubhouse, Norwich in 1914.

Thorpe Station was built to resemble a country house and it looks almost exactly the same today as it did during the war when it saw thousands of troops depart for the front. It was also continuously used by the Red Cross.

Ryburgh, some 20 miles north-west of Norwich. Many joined up in the same week and, because they worked together in the foundry or the malting or on farms, they went as Pals. This little village lost twenty-three men altogether, including two brothers, Albert and Frederick Green.

On 2 September more than 100 men marched through Norwich to Blackfriars Hall to enlist. This was a Pals battalion, 'the Business Men's Company', which became the 8th Norfolks.

On 8 August the *Norwich Mercury* carried a report on men signing up in the small village of Hilgay:

> The whole of the population turned out to see the stalwarts off, and there were some pathetic scenes. One family had given four sons, and several three. Headed by the Hilgay Excelsior Brass Band, the little soldiers marched to Downham Station… While waiting for the train, the band played *Rule Britannia, Auld Lang Syne* and the National Anthem.

In all, the Hilgay War Memorial lists a total of thirty-eight men who died for king and country during the course of the conflict.

Wymondham is a picturesque town just under 10 miles south of Norwich and paid a heavy price in lives lost, over 140. One man who did survive was the local barber. He put up a sign in his shop: 'Closed. Gone to join my group. Shall reopen after victory.' He duly did.

Recruitment was no doubt helped by the reports of the German Emperor's appeal to his own people:

> Therefore to Arms! Any dallying, any temporizing, would be to betray the Fatherland. To be or not to be, is the question for the Empire which our fathers founded. To be or not to be German power and German existence. We shall resist to the last breath of man and horse, and shall fight out the struggle even against a world of enemies.

Meeting in St Andrew's Hall

On 31 August Ian Malcolm MP led a recruitment drive culminating in a mass meeting in Norwich's St Andrew's Hall. As chance would have it, this gathering coincided with the end of the harvest and encouraging news from local industry. On the day of the meeting, a letter was

Men leave Norwich to sign up and receive an enthusiastic send-off.

New recruits marching up towards the Guildhall in Norwich, 1914.

published in the *Eastern Evening News* from Norwich brewery Steward and Patteson stating that any of its workers joining the 'New Army' would have their jobs kept open for them with assistance offered to their dependants. Men thronged into St Andrew's Hall with many unable to get in. To the *Evening News* it seemed as if almost all of Norwich was there that night: 250 men signed up there and then, another 1,000 the next day and 2,500 within a week.

At Mattishall, twenty-four volunteers had a communal breakfast and signed on together at Dereham recruiting office.

Britannia Barracks overlooking the city.

Many pictures of marching men show them in suits and caps: this is not just because they were yet to sign up but also because the rush to enlist was so great that there was a severe shortage of uniforms for a while.

The army grew in size from 386,000 on 4 August to 825,000 by 9 September. By 11 September it was reported that some 300 men had additionally enrolled at the Britannia Barracks.

A message from the king
In August 1914 as British troops started leaving for war, the king sent this message to them:

> You are leaving home to fight for the safety and honour of my Empire. Belgium, whose country we are pledged to defend has been attacked and France is about to be invaded by the same powerful foe. I have implicit confidence in you, my soldiers. Duty is your watchword and I know your duty will be nobly done.

Essex Regiment having hair cut in Norwich Market Place, 1914.

The Market Place from Gentleman's Walk today. In the background, left to right: the Sir Garnet pub and St Peter Mancroft Church, both there during the Great War; the Forum and the 'new' Town Hall that were opened in 2002 and 1938 respectively.

I shall follow your every movement with deepest interest and mark with eager satisfaction your daily progress: indeed, your welfare will never be absent from my thoughts.

I pray God to bless you and guard you and bring you back victorious.

Cyclist battalions

British military cyclists date from around 1887. They were originally seen as complementary to the cavalry and were nicknamed 'the Gas Pipe Cavalry'. The first wholly Norfolk battalion was formed in 1908, Lord Coke telling the War Office that Norfolk men were the finest cyclists in England.

One man, when asked by an officer the advantages of a cyclist compared to an infantryman, replied: 'They don't have to walk.' In fact this was how the cyclist battalion was seen: as mounted infantrymen, using the cycle only as a means of travelling from one place to another. In 1908 the 1st Battalion, Norfolk Volunteers Infantry Brigade consisted of 4 officers and 176 non-commissioned officers who had been transferred from the defunct Volunteer Force. Pay was 1s per day, a one-off payment for each tour of 3s for wear and tear on boots, and £1 for every eight days a man used his own bicycle.

Recruits needed to be aged between 17 and 35 with a minimum chest measurement of 33 inches and not less than 5ft 2in tall. There was a signing-up period of four years. The men were well kitted out with a service uniform and one for walking out that included a smart blue cap and frock coat. They shared Norwich Drill Hall with the Norfolk Yeomanry. When war broke out, these men patrolled the Norfolk and Suffolk coast.

The Half-Crown Holy Boys

It soon became clear that another battalion was needed and a second was formed. They were known as the 2/6th or 'half-crown boys' (2s/6d was half-a-crown in old money, a crown being five shillings). As they

Rushing to give the troops refreshment, St Augustine's.

were from Norwich, known for being a city with lots of churches, they also gained the nickname 'Holy Boys'. For the rest of the war they gloried in the name 'the Half-Crown Holy Boys'. They did not, however, stay in Norfolk: they were posted to protect the Yorkshire coast and lasting bonds were formed between the two areas that last to this day. A further battalion, the 3/6th, was formed in 1915.

Nearly all of the 1st and some of the Half-Crown Holy Boys were subsequently sent overseas. Colonel Prior, the prime mover in the formation of the 1st Battalion, assumed command of the 9th Battalion, Norfolk Regiment in France in 1916. He survived the conflict but not without being gassed and wounded on several occasions. He twice received the Distinguished Service Order and died in 1953.

The Peppermint Boys
The name derives from the black and white caps of the boys – which reminded people of peppermints – from Bracondale School, a fine school that was situated on a Norwich ridge overlooking the River Wensum. Many of the boys joined the 8th Battalion of the Norfolk Regiment which was in the thick of the action at the Somme. Several were killed. Forty-four former pupils gave their lives in the First World War and their names are listed on the school's War Memorial. It helps to put these numbers in context when bearing in mind that the total number of men raised by the Norfolk Regiment during the war was 32,375. More than one in six of these young men died.

The oldest and first of the Bracondale boys to die was Captain Charles Norman Wheeler, born in 1881 and son of the headmaster, Dr Francis Darkins Wheeler. He died in January 1915, aged 33, on the first day in the trenches, having been shot in the head. His nickname among his students was 'Pop'. One of the youngest was Flight Lieutenant Myer Joseph Levine of Norwich, just 18 years old. He was flying from Mousehold and crashed over Lincolnshire.

Another flyer was Captain Donald Charles Cunnell. He was born at Mount Pleasant, Norwich and his father, Charles, was a brick manufacturer. Just days before his death in 1917 he and his gunner, Albert Woodridge, had shot down the legendary flying ace Manfred von Richthofen, known as the Red Baron. The latter survived but was injured and never regained his former fitness before finally being shot down and killed on 21 April 1918. Cunnell himself was killed just a week after his encounter with the Red Baron, hit by artillery shells when returning to base on 12 July 1917. He was 23 years old.

David Alexander Glen of Norwich was a popular and talented flyer. After leaving Bracondale he joined the Royal Flying Corps and was awarded the Croix de Guerre for gallantry. In December 1915 he was shot down and killed over German lines. He was escorting Lieutenant William Sholto Douglas (later chief of the RAF) on reconnaissance as far as Cambrai and St Quentin when they saw six enemy planes heading towards them. He was aged just 19.

Memorial in Norwich Cathedral to boys and masters of the Boys' Model School, Norwich who 'gave their lives in defence of right'. The school was wound up in 1920.

Several sets of brothers also died.

The art of flying was so new and the planes so delicate that many young men died before facing the enemy. One such was Lieutenant William Miles, born in Norwich, who died in training later on 24 July 1918 at Reading. Of the 14,000 pilots who died in the Great War, 8,000 were killed in training. Among those who reached the front, life expectancy was often just a few weeks.

Heigham Woodbine Willie

One remarkable man who enlisted immediately was The Reverend Samuel Frederick Leighton Green, known affectionately to his parishioners after the war as Heigham Woodbine Willie. He was vicar of St Bartholomew, Heigham in Norwich. He was given a commission, serving on the Western Front as chaplain to a unit of EastEnders from London who became devoted to him and he to them. He regularly wrote home to his Norwich parishioners who, although among the poorest in the city, regularly sent him magazines and cigarettes for the unit. He underwent gassing, poisoning and trench fever and was awarded two Military Crosses. After the war he suffered a breakdown but was able to accept a living on the Norfolk coast at All Saints, Mundesley. He died in 1929, aged just 47, and was buried with full military honours.

Norwich Police

In February 1915 John Gordon-Munn, Lord Mayor of Norwich, formed three Royal Engineer Field Companies that were Pals units. These were the 207th, 208th and 209th field companies that went on to combine with the 34th Division of the British army which subsequently suffered terrible casualties. Seven police officers signed up for the 208th. As part of the 34th Division, the men were in France by 15 January 1916 and their first experience of battle was a bloodbath. The 34th Division lost 6,811 men between 1 and 5 July 1916, only three of the police Pals surviving the war and returning to duties in Norwich.

Norwich Union

All employees who signed up were guaranteed their jobs back and had their pay supplemented to the amount that they earned with the company.

Initially the outlook for business looked bleak but quickly recovered, helped by many people and companies who no longer wanted German insurance policies. Also the government became a large customer as it was keen to insure against compensation for war damage. Being subject to much enemy bombardment, the War Risk Insurance for Norfolk was enormous. A special watch was kept for enemy Zeppelins from the top of the Surrey Street Headquarters. The German press many times wrote of the destruction of this building but George Skipper's masterpiece survives unscathed to this day.

In total 551 men joined up, 87 per cent of those eligible; very high indeed. Of these, sixty-four men never returned and thirty-six were decorated for valour.

Lights

In pre-war days, the glow from the lights of Norwich at night could be seen out at sea between Yarmouth and Palling and on the marsh level from the coast at Horsey. Around the middle of October 1914, the Norwich Police received a complaint that the glare of lights from the city was plainly visible at Happisburgh, a distance of 25 miles away. It was considered by authorities in Norwich – although opinion was expressed in other major towns such as King's Lynn and Ipswich that the reaction was 'over the top' – that steps must be taken to reduce the lights.

At first, suggestions were not obligatory. In early November the police said that all lights in front of retail establishments should be either extinguished or at least shielded. As no one paid much attention, however, the Officer Commanding Troops in Norwich re-issued instructions as an order. It was further decreed that all trams, as well as trains, should travel with blinds down. The lights on the tops of the trams were blacked out and a week later all shop lights were shaded black and red. This turned Norwich into a 'city of dreadful night', according to some. Ipswich by contrast had made no arrangements for shading lights. This action on the part of Norwich was seen to be justified in the first Zeppelin attack on 19 January 1915, when Lynn and Yarmouth suffered very badly. In the region's capital city, precautions were taken as soon as the Zeppelins were sighted off Bacton and although one on its return journey passed over the northern part of Norwich, the city remained invisible from the air. Fortunately, it was also a night when mists rose up from the Yare and Wensum valleys.

Anti-German sentiment

Germans in Britain – and their businesses – were targeted. Prime Minister Asquith had to fight to prevent his family's German governess being questioned. Many people – including, laughably, composer Ralph Vaughan Williams – were suspected of being German spies. There was a widespread feeling that anyone of German descent should be rounded up and if it was seen that a previous idea to send them to a 'colony' was unrealistic, then at least they should be kept under guard.

One German guest house owner in Sheringham, Jacob Lichter, brought a court case against people who had booked into his

German prisoners in the Market Place, 1914. The statue of His Grace the Duke of Wellington has now been moved to Cathedral Close.

establishment but failed to turn up after war broke out. This was a great mistake on his part as Judge Mulligan of North Walsham County Court threw the case out, adding some scathing remarks about the absurdity of allowing Germans to run guest houses on the vulnerable Norfolk coast. Lichter was far from alone, however, as the letters' page of local newspapers makes plain: many hotel and guest house owners sought some form of compensation, faced with probable ruin if the war lasted any length of time.

The Archbishop of York, Cosmo Gordon Lang, spoke out against anti-German feelings.

Spies everywhere
Spies were seen by some people in every nook and cranny. The MP for King's Lynn, Holcombe Ingleby, suggested after the first Zeppelin raids that a specially-trained group of car-owners were directing the airships by using their lights. Other people thought that houses on the coast were using lights to signal to German U-boats.

Famous in his time for 'making safe' much of the north Norfolk coastline was Major Egbert Napier, Chief Constable of the Norfolk County Constabulary, who spent a great deal of his time hunting spies. He subsequently signed up into the Royal Garrison Artillery and was killed in October 1917.

At the beginning of November 1914, Carl Hans Lody was executed by firing squad at the Tower of London for being a German spy. It was the first execution at the Tower since 1747.

The Red Cross
Before the war the local Red Cross was split up into detachments, the women's containing about thirty staff and the men's fifty. In 1914 the men were asked to transport the wounded from Thorpe Station to the Norfolk and Norwich Hospital. An additional 120 men were recruited, and this later rose to about 200. The four men's detachments were formed into the Norwich Transport Company that served as a model for other cities. The company dealt in total with 322 convoys and more than 41,000 men.

The men also had additional duties during air-raids when they were in charge of first-aid appliances. Fortunately no bombs fell on Norwich as it turned out, due in very large part to the total blackouts during Zeppelin raids.

The men also ran a Rest Hut at Thorpe Station that was used by over 25,000 troops. A few divisions were charged with taking the wounded off the trains and transporting them to hospital. The County Director, Lieutenant Colonel G.H. Thompson, expressed the opinion that the Norwich Transport Company was the most efficient in England and it was honourably demobilized in May 1919.

Four ambulances were sent to Norwich by the British Red Cross Society; the Clergy Ambulance and three privately-owned ambulances also operated there. In addition, private cars were used to transport men with lesser injuries.

Two new women's detachments were formed during the war, and of the five existing detachments, two ran Town Close Hospital between them. This was for local patients and did not receive Expeditionary Force men. The Commandant was Mrs Mahon who had previously run the hospital in Cathedral Close.

There was also Bracondale Hospital run by Miss Montgomery and Norfolk 66 Voluntary Aid Detachment. This took Expeditionary Force men. There were two more hospitals: Carrow Auxiliary Hospital and the Bishop's Palace Hospital, although these were not under the jurisdiction of the Norwich Division. Lakenham School, which had just been completed, was turned into a hospital with 100 beds and became a military institution run by the army. Ingham Old Hall was an auxiliary war hospital from 29 October 1914 to 28 January 1919. The

Annexe ward in a Norfolk hospital.

commandant of the Ingham War Hospital was Sarah Gamzu Gurney, MBE. In total 1,082 patients were admitted, usually to convalesce after a serious injury or illness.

Nursing

Nursing could be an exhausting duty. The nurses had everyday responsibility for care of the wounded: washing, cleaning and administering medicines. Prior to working, they had to pass exams in both first aid and nursing. However, medical equipment of the time was basic. For example, sometimes only saline was available as a disinfectant for cleaning wounds, equipment and furniture alike.

A small daily allowance was paid to the nurses, but training and uniforms were usually paid for by the girls themselves and a nurse had to sew on her own red cross. Once appointed, the volunteers could only claim travel, board and laundry expenses.

A great shock: three British ships sunk in ninety minutes

A great jolt to people's confidence in the dominance of the Royal Navy was felt when, on 22 September 1914, three of her ships went down in ninety minutes, sunk by German U-boat *U-9*. Norfolk men, including eleven from King's Lynn and others from Norfolk coastal communities were among those lost.

It was on the morning of 22 September that *Aboukir* and her sister ships *Cressy* and *Hogue* were on patrol without any escorting destroyers. They were not expecting submarine attack, but they had lookouts posted and one gun manned on each side to attack any submarines sighted. They were sailing at about 10 knots when they were spotted by the German submarine *U-9*, commanded by *Kapitnleutnant* Otto Weddigen, and on surfacing she moved to attack. She fired one torpedo at 06:20 at *Aboukir*. *Hogue* was struck about half an hour later and sank within twenty minutes. *Cressy* attempted to ram the submarine as it surfaced but failed to hit as *U-9* dived again. *Cressy* resumed her rescue efforts but was torpedoed within minutes of *Hogue* going down and sank thirty minutes later.

Several Dutch ships were in the vicinity, along with British fishing trawlers including two vessels from Lowestoft. Skipper Thomas Phillips was hailed as a hero for braving what he thought was a minefield to pick up more than 150 survivors from the three cruisers.

A German postcard celebrating the 'Victories of U-9*'.*

HMS Aboukir.

Together with fellow Lowestoft fisherman George Jacobs, he was subsequently awarded the Sea Gallantry Medal for his rescue work. More than half of the three ships' 2,100 men were lost, but between them the two men saved more than 400. The British government authorized salvage of the wrecks in 2011.

Sports
War broke out at the start of Norwich Cricket Week, where the county side ended the first day of their match against Hertfordshire at Lakenham with a 99-run lead. The *Eastern Daily Press* was, on the day after declaration of hostilities, full of news of the matches taking place at all levels, including one between Sheringham Visitors and Gresham High School Masters. Soon, however, none other than the great W.G. Grace suggested that it was inappropriate for cricket to continue. On 31 December the paper carried a letter from C.B.I. Prior, Honorary Secretary to the Norfolk Cricket Association: 'Dear Sir, I agree with the letter of Dr WG Grace... that cricket should be stopped, and that cricketers should do their duty to their King and country.'

Nevertheless, cricket did continue among the troops as it was seen as good for morale. It was particularly useful in helping men recover from the effects of war. One example, reported on 9 June 1916, was a match between the Norfolk War Hospital and the Norfolk Regiment. The hospital made a total of 93 but was outplayed by the regiment which made 184 and this despite Dr McCall taking 6 for 28 on behalf of the hospital.

With football, it was a similar story. Initially, Lord Kinnaird, President of the FA, said that organized football should continue as it was good for morale. In reality, as in all sports, many men joined up with their friends in Pals' battalions. One of these was Norwich's captain, Jock MacKenzie, who became a lance corporal in the Royal Garrison Artillery. He had a distinguished military career, earning two medals, survived the war and died in 1940 aged 55. Another was Philip Fullard who went to King Edward VI School in Norwich and learned to fly 'as a gentleman', i.e. at his own expense. He joined the Royal Flying Corps and had forty 'kills' before ironically breaking his leg playing football and this marked the end of his war service.

At this time Norwich played in the Southern League Division One and their ground was at The Nest on Rosary Road, a couple of miles from their current fine stadium at Carrow Road. The 1914 season saw them finish fourteenth out of twenty teams that included West Ham and Crystal Palace. The war was disastrous for the team financially as they had spiralling debts and no income, going into voluntary liquidation in 1919.

The Five Nations Rugby tournament was suspended until 1920, the last pre-war match taking place between England and Scotland in March 1914. England won 16–15.

On a more positive note, the war led to a huge increase in women's sport, especially football, as the firms employing them in place of men who had gone to the front saw the benefits in morale that resulted from a vigorous sporting schedule.

Christmas truce 1914
The most famous football match of the war took place on the front lines. In the well-documented Christmas truce of 1914 an impromptu football kick-about ensued between the two front lines for about an hour and a half. Gifts were exchanged, such as pipe tobacco and chocolate. According to one report, a Christmas carol, sung in German to an English tune, drifted across the lines and was taken up by most of the troops. In the Castle Museum, Norwich is a long silver whistle, gifted to the Royal Norfolk Regiment and now encased in a glass frame, the description of which reads: 'This whistle was played by Sergeant E.C. Hoy on Christmas morning 1914, the occasion of the unofficial truce on the Western Front around Ypres.'

Some Norwich men wrote home that the enemy troops looked unhappy and without any enthusiasm for the fight, and they thought the war could soon be over.

The truce itself lasted until the end of the month in some places, but this was a very inconsistent situation. It is reported that, as midnight approached on Christmas Day, a message was received from the Germans to say that they would unfortunately have to resume firing at midnight but would aim high; nonetheless, would the English troops please keep their heads down anyway to avoid any accidents.

The 38th Wimbledon Championships took place at the end of June and beginning of July 1914. It was thereafter decided to suspend the championships for the duration of the war.

CHAPTER 3

1915:
Deepening Conflict

1915 at a glance

• 19–20 January: Great Yarmouth and King's Lynn attacked by Zeppelins in first such raid of the war; four people killed.

• 18 February: Germany begins U-boat blockade of Great Britain.

• 10 March: Allies suffer 12,800 losses in offensive at Neuve Chapelle. Many question the quality of British shells. Harry Daniels, born in Wymondham, Norfolk, wins Victoria Cross in battle.

• 22 April: Second Battle of Ypres. Germans experiment with poison gas for first time.

• 25 April: Gallipoli landings.

• 7 May: German submarine sinks British liner *Lusitania*.

• 25 May: Widespread discontent over conduct of war; coalition government formed.

• 12 August: 5th Norfolks launch disastrous attack at Gallipoli. One of the units that suffered heavy losses was made up of Sandringham estate workers.

• 9 September: Dereham attacked by Zeppelins.

• 12 October: Edith Cavell, having been tried entirely in German which she did not understand, executed by firing squad.

• 20 December: Some 83,000 allied troops evacuated from Gallipoli; evacuation of Helles followed two weeks later.

How was life in Norwich?

In various respects, daily life in Norwich continued as always. In May the *Evening News* was advertising Wincarnis for those who were 'weak, nervy, and rundown'. In the same month it reported that the production of *David Copperfield* at the Theatre Royal was 'excellent'. Scott's Emulsion was 'The builder-up children love', and in order to really enjoy life you needed 'Dr Matthews Liver and Stomach pills'. In September the *Evening News* reminded readers: 'Toothless we came into the world and, more often than not, toothless we leave it, but there is no reason to remain toothless all the time. London Dental, Castle St, Norwich. Complete sets from £.1s. Gold and Vulcanite £3.3s.' Shoppers were, however, given advice to make life easier in the current circumstances: shop as early as possible; do not expect immediate service during busy periods; put your requirements in writing before shopping if possible; and do not expect to have goods delivered always but be prepared to carry them home yourself.

The courts continued to be busy. On 16 April at Shirehall a landlady was summonsed for allowing beer to be served to two civilians and eight soldiers after 9:30 in defiance of closing regulations. An Erpingham farmer was fined for employing two boys; in each case a 24s fine or, in default, 13 days' imprisonment. There were scenes of discontent on the streets of Catton as the good people of that area had greatly enjoyed their role until then of housing and feeding UK troops and appealed against the decision to house them in another part of the city. The army took to the letters' pages of the local press to explain the decision and refused to rescind it.

Double loss for Dereham family

A Dereham family lost two brothers within a few days of each other. Private Percy Thurgill of the 1st Battalion, Norfolk Regiment was killed in action in Flanders on or about 18 April 1915. His elder brother, Stephen, was killed in Basra on 22 April.

Edith Cavell

The most celebrated citizen of the Fine City who died in this year was probably Nurse Edith Cavell. She was born in Swardeston, just outside Norwich, where her father was vicar for forty-five years. She was a small woman of strong religious convictions who told her fellow nurses

Edith Cavell.

in occupied Belgium that it was their duty to tend anyone who was wounded or ill, irrespective of nationality. 'There are two sides to war,' she remarked, 'the glory and the misery.'

Edith Cavell helped many a wounded soldier escape to the UK and other countries. In 1915 she was arrested, tried entirely in German – a language she did not understand – and executed by a German firing squad on 12 October. On the night before her death, she famously remarked that 'Patriotism is not enough', as she would willingly have helped any soldier. After the war she was reburied at the east side of Norwich Cathedral.

There is a fine memorial to her just outside the Erpingham Gate which leads into the Anglican Cathedral (the gate is named after another Norwich hero, Sir Thomas Erpingham, who led the victorious archers at the Battle of Agincourt: look up to see a statue of him in prayer, thanking God for having saved his life). Almost opposite, there is a pub bearing Edith Cavell's name.

She is still very much a figure of discussion today, partly because a legend has grown up around her. Why, ask some, when caught did she attend court in day clothes, not in nursing uniform – which may have elicited some sympathy – and refuse to lie or hide the truth? Why was she not more careful? Today there is a campaign to issue a banknote of the realm – possibly a £20 one – to commemorate her courage. In any event her death was of immense propaganda value to the allies, some claiming that as many as 40,000 additional men signed up to fight 'the savage Hun' as a direct result.

The Volunteers become more professional

Early in 1915 the much-derided Volunteer Training Corps were renamed City of Norwich Volunteers. Each of four battalions had their own cyclist, ambulance and signalling sections. They were issued with red brassards (armbands) with the letters 'G.R.' ('Georgius Rex') on them that provided amused and often rude speculation among the public as to what this might stand for. On Sunday afternoons they met in the Market Place before marching around the town in various directions. At Easter a bugle band was started and fifty Martini rifles were purchased. The public was slowly beginning to value them and an appeal for £4,000 for equipment met with a generous response.

Most Norfolk towns and many villages set up their own Volunteer Corps and the Norwich Volunteers became the 1st Battalion, the War Office approving a badge that was the City of Norwich arms without the supporters. The numbers were swelled by men of military age who were granted exemption from active service provided they joined the Volunteers.

They were put to work. The Volunteers found work at the aerodrome at Bacton and in preparing the airship station at Pulham. For many months Volunteers from all over Norfolk took the train to Pulham St Mary Station and then marched to the aerodrome, preceded by their band. Locals lined the route to see the spectacle. Their work

Chapelfield Gardens were used as a training ground for the Volunteers. Some 500 years earlier the same site had been used for practice by the archers who were to win the Battle of Agincourt under their commander, Sir Thomas Erpingham.

was basic but essential: tending hedges, filling ditches, clearing trees and digging for railway tracks connecting the site to Pulham Market.

Perhaps the most important part of their duties was patrolling stretches of railway line from nine or ten at night until six in the morning. The Norwich men were mostly engaged in patrol work from Keswick to Brundall, on the Cromer line near Whitlingham and in guarding the swing bridge at Trowse.

A highlight of December 1915 was 'The Battle of Caistor' when the Volunteers were split into two 'armies', one told to force through the lines at Markshall and the other to 'hold'. There was a great deal of noise but the only casualty was a rabbit that one of the 'attackers' accidentally fell on and killed.

Further drastic action on Norwich lights and gas

On 23 January 1915, 6,000 handbills of a lighting order were printed and distributed by Special Constables to houses in the city. This was one of the first major tasks for the Specials and was enthusiastically carried out by several hundred of them.

Three days later Brigadier General Daniel issued a more stringent order whereby all lights visible outside a building were to be extinguished between 5.30 pm and 7 am. Only a few lamps were lit on the city streets and on main highways. It was also announced that in the event of a further enemy attack electricity would be cut off at the power station. People were advised to turn off the gas at the mains and remain on the ground floor or in the cellar of their houses. Further raids were seen as almost inevitable and so evening classes were abandoned, drills by the Volunteer Training Corps stopped and all factory production ceased at 5 pm. No shops were open after dark either.

Thereafter, further drastic steps were ordered by the Home Office: for example, all lights in trams were forbidden, only a single candle being allowed. This practice was soon changed as it made travelling by tram extremely perilous; thereafter trams were allowed one shaded interior light provided the blinds were completely drawn. Headlights and top-lights were darkened. All the new state-of-the-art street lighting was turned off, although for a short time a blue light was permitted on dangerous corners but this was quickly abandoned.

Householders pasted strips of dark paper down the sides of their windows, shaded electric lights and gas globes and pasted opaque paper over fanlights. Factories with fanlights found it necessary to make elaborate arrangements for these to be covered nightly with tarpaulins. Fines were imposed on citizens who did not co-operate, magistrates vastly increasing the fines for a subsequent offence. Newsboys, tram conductors and others used bull's-eye lanterns. Car headlights were also affected. Cyclists adopted many makeshifts and local writer W.G. Clarke remarked: '…I saw acetylene lamps with handkerchiefs tied over them, and ordinary stable lanterns with candles, laboriously fastened to the front lamp bracket.' The kerbs in the main streets were whitened to improve their visibility.

On 20 September 1915, the Home Secretary ordered that the regulations for lighting should apply from half an hour after sunset to half an hour before sunrise and this remained in force until the end of the war. From November even the striking of matches became an offence, for which many were fined. Norwich had become the darkest city in the land, a 'City of Dreadful Night'. Some protested that it was unnecessary but to no avail.

Humour in the darkness

Even on these nights of extreme darkness, there were comic moments. Some citizens were unable to find their own homes, or feeling sure that they could not be mistaken, boldly walked into someone else's house. Ladies who needed to go a short distance in the street lost their bearings and had to enquire where they were. Pedestrians walked into trees, lampposts or street orderly bins and tripped over kerbs. For some it was nerve-wracking to hear footsteps behind them but unable to see who was there. Worse, some carried umbrellas and slashed them about in front of them to clear their path as if sword-fighting with an imaginary foe. Luminous discs were a partial answer but injury frequently resulted nevertheless.

One other consequence of the darkness, according to the weekly paper the *Norfolk Chronicle*, was that people had begun to read more serious books as they stayed at home. The paper observed that the Scots had always been serious about their literature.

Fines for showing a light

To begin with, police and magistrates were unwilling to prosecute people for breaking the lighting regulations. From March 1915, however, to the end of the war, 1,028 summonses were dealt with and fines inflicted amounting to £379 6s; before the end of the war the total number of people summonsed for offences against the lighting regulations was 4,042 and the total amount of fines inflicted was £1,357 10s 7d.

Some famous firms

As remarked in Chapter 1, Norwich was an Edwardian industrial powerhouse with some of its firms making a priceless contribution to the war effort. One such was Howlett and White. Before the war the firm made women's fine satin and brocade dress shoes. Upon the outbreak of war, the company offered their services to the War Office and contracted to make army boots. The first shipment was for the French army and were the first army boots ever made in Norwich. Then they made the brogue shoe as used by Highland regiments in the early part of the war. In addition, the regulation British army boot – a Derby style with uppers of black chrome calf or russet kip – and the magnificent British field service boot with high legs, lacing to within six inches of the top and then secured with three straps and buckles just below the knee, were all made in very large quantities by the firm. They were without comparison anywhere in the world.

The firm was subsequently requested to make both the Russian ankle-boot and the Cossack boot. The former was a Derby-style boot and the latter a pull-on boot coming up to the knee and secured by a strap and buckle at the top. The men who wore these boots must have been extremely large in stature, for the Russian a 7B size, the smallest, was equal to a size 10 in the British regulation boot. Some wit called them the 'Russian Boats'. These contracts were placed and paid for by the British government. The company also made very heavy Italian Alpine boots.

A famous Norwich brand.

The very elegant building in Colegate that originally housed Howlett and White, now partly the Jane Austen College and a variety of businesses.

However, the most interesting of the firm's productions was, undoubtedly, the Royal Air Force boot. This aviation thigh boot was made of sheepskin with the wool inside, fastened at the hip with a strap and buckle, also at the knee and at the instep. It had rubber soles.

In addition there were various contracts for felt slippers, canvas fatigue shoes and shoes for the Women's Army Auxiliary Corps abroad. Also large quantities of shoes were made for the navy.

For a time tradesmen were to be found working side-by-side on delicate brocade silk evening shoes and on heavy army boots.

Production figures for the war were as follows:

Boots and shoes for the British armies: 453,000 pairs
Boots for the allies: 32,000 pairs
British Aviation boots. 21,000 pairs

At the end of the war the company produced the Norvic Shoe de Luxe for ladies, Norvic being a famous name that existed right up to the 1980s in every High Street. Unfortunately, they then lost a massive contract and within a short time all their shops were sold to try to make up the deficit.

Another major boot and shoe manufacturer was Edwards and Holmes. This firm began in 1891 in a four-room cottage in Pottergate Street where the rent was 3s 6d a week. They then moved to St George's, thereafter to Botolph Street and in 1896 to a purpose-built factory in Esdelle Street.

Prior to the war they exported mainly to South Africa and Australia, but this became impossible with the advent of the German U-boat menace. Thus they set about making shoes for the British people and produced 120,000 pairs during the war. Many ingenious substitutes for leather were tried. Some 367 men signed up from the company, 46 of whom died.

'That Norwich played an important part in equipping our men and those of our Allies with large quantities of boots and shoes is a matter for the greatest congratulation,' declared the press in 1919. During the war the firm of P. Haldinstein and Sons supplied over half a million pairs of boots and shoes from Norwich factories and an equal number for the allies. The firm was founded in 1799 by David Solman from French Alsace who was then joined by a Norwich man, Mr Philip Haldinstein.

As the war progressed, 90 per cent of the men signed up and new women employees had to be rapidly trained. All jobs were kept open for the men and at the end of the war many of them went back to work for the firm. These women workers were exceptionally generous in providing funds for comforts and entertainments at the local hospitals.

In 1919 the firm was exporting, or had exported, to over fifty-six countries and colonies, and expanded from their premises in Princes Street and Queen Street towards Tombland. Frank Haldinstein, son of the firm's owner, attended Norwich Grammar School and Christ Church, Oxford. He was a captain in the Royal Engineers and died on 7 March 1917 aged just 22 as a result of wounds sustained at the Somme.

A turnshoe firm was Sexton, Son and Everard. Formed only in 1913, by the end of the war this firm employed 550 people. It was situated in St Mary's Works in Oak Street, a building of 39,000 square feet that could house 700 workers. They specialized in the turnshoe trade, meaning that the shoes were made inside out and 'turned' after the soles had been applied to the uppers.

Sexton, Son and Everard still have their crest over the front door of their original factory building on Oak Street, now occupied by various businesses.

The company was an enormous boon to the area, as this part of town was one of the very poorest, the site of many of the notorious Norwich 'yards'. By 1919 they specialized in Louis heel goods, with exceptionally high heels utilizing coloured fancy leathers.

S.L. Witton was a well-known shoe manufacturer, mainly based in Muspole Street but also in Colegate and St George Street, and 150 of their men signed up. Prior to the war they were producing over 10,000 pairs of children's shoes a week.

Finally, regarding shoes and boots, mention must be made of Wm Hurrell, Phoenix Works, Magdalen Street. Their first order from the government was for 40,000 pairs of shoes for military rest camps and hospitals. So well-made were they that only six pairs were returned. Some 154 company men joined up and just 3 were killed. Mr William Hurrell, the proprietor, received a commission in the Royal Flying Corps and was awarded the Distinguished Flying Cross for bravery over France. They were famous after the conflict for the 'Cinema' brand of children's shoes.

A firm of a different type, and critical to the war effort, was Boulton & Paul, situated on Riverside. Perhaps their greatest contribution was producing more of the Sopwith Camel aircraft than anyone else; these were tested out on Mousehold Heath. Bolton and Paul was originally founded in 1797 when William Moore, aged 33, of Warham came to Norwich and opened an ironmonger's shop in Cockey Lane. A few years later he took into partnership John Hilling Barnard, naming the firm Moore & Barnard, ironmongers and stove grate manufacturers. Their shop sat on the corner of Little London Street, facing London Street, later the site of Garlands' store.

In 1865 a small factory was opened in Rose Lane and Dawson Paul was made manager at a salary of £100 per year with a house provided within the factory grounds, rent and rates free. Three years later Boulton sold the ironmongery business to Messrs Piper & Theobald (later Johnson, Burton & Theobald), and devoted all his energies to the manufacturing part of the concern in Rose Lane.

The firm rapidly became expert in practically anything made of metal. They made agricultural and horticultural implements, strained wire fencing, iron hurdles, park gates, garden chairs, iron bedsteads, kitchen ranges, hot-water apparatus, and mincing and sausage machines. They subsequently constructed complete iron dwellings and even a lighthouse in Brazil.

Modern sculptures commemorating Boulton & Paul on Riverside. As can be seen in the background, the site of the original works now consists of flats.

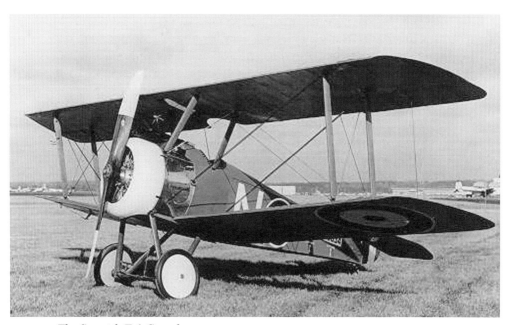

The Sopwith F-1 Camel.

The year 1868 was very important as it saw a significant technological innovation with the installation of wire netting machines. There was an almost limitless demand for wire netting to control rabbits in Australia. The firm started with three machines producing 2ft, 3ft and 4ft-wide netting respectively. The looms were constructed almost entirely of wood and were extremely difficult to use. They had to work day and night in order to keep up with the demand. A year later Dawson Paul was taken into partnership and the firm renamed Boulton & Paul.

In the 1880s another Barnard joined the firm. John Neville Barnard, son of a builder and not related to the original partners of the same name, had received his training at Howes & Son, engineers. He then joined the firm of Smithdale & Sons. At this time the works was gaining international recognition along with new orders, especially in the wire netting department, and Barnard succeeded in designing much more efficient wire netting machinery.

Boulton & Paul became a Limited Company on 14 December 1897, with J.J. Dawson Paul as governing director and Henry ffiske, who had been made a partner four years previously, as managing director.

They supplied 1,500ft of piping for the Plantation Garden in Norwich. They also built aviaries, complete suburban bungalows and iron bridges. Young Dawson Paul and Geoffrey ffiske are also credited with making a boat called the 'Dollydo' that was so successful in racing that no one was prepared to take it on. In 1910 they constructed the sledges for Robert Falcon Scott's ill-fated second expedition to the Antarctic.

Some of the first orders on the outbreak of war were a naval hospital at Dover, huts and stables for 6,000 men and horses, a prisoner-of-war camp in Jersey, hangars for the Royal Flying Corps, steel-framed buildings in arsenals and dockyards, hospitals in France and warehouses in Mesopotamia. The Fencing Department began making field kitchens and the Engine Department made electric lighting plant. After the war, projects of a basically wooden frame became the norm but this was undoubtedly the great age of iron and steel.

Perhaps their greatest moment came in 1915 when they were asked to make aeroplanes. William ffiske took charge of the commercial side of the project, while Stanley Howes (of Howes & Sons, Engineers who had also wanted to help with the war effort) agreed to undertake the

The site of Boulton & Paul today, now riverside flats.

erection and assembly of the aircraft. Eventually some 2,000 people were employed in this way at the Rose Lane Works. The first aeroplane was ready by October 1915 and buildings were quickly erected on Mousehold Heath, overlooking the city.

Altogether they made 550 F.E.s, 1,550 Sopwith Camels, and later Snipes, a modification of the Camel. In all 2,530 military aircraft were completed. Boulton & Paul's chief aircraft designer was John Dudley North (1893–1968), who joined the company from Austin Motor Company Aircraft Department.

In collaboration with other East Anglian firms they made shells, and a company, Norwich Components Ltd, was set up to manufacture fuses. It produced more than 2 million and when, as reported later, the old warehouse in which it operated was burned to the ground in 1917, they took over the city's skating rink. The firm thrived for generations after the war; eventually, after a series of mergers, becoming Dowty Aerospace. It became the TI group in 1992.

Norwich was also central to the production of clothing, both for civilians and troops. One famous firm was Chamberlins, with a factory in Botolph Street. All production was switched in just one month from civilian and home goods to supplies for the Admiralty and War Office.

The firm produced the khaki clothing for all the Norfolk Territorial units and various Volunteer battalions. They also were sole suppliers to Great Britain and the colonies of Pegamoid waterproof clothing and the vast bulk of this went to the war effort. Also supplies of the firm's East Coast oilskin waterproof material were in such demand that the entire output was requisitioned by the War Office and Admiralty, a new factory being built to cope with demand.

Suits were also made for discharged soldiers. In total the company made close on 1 million garments. One of the directors sat on the Advisory Board to advise on clothing for the troops, while 125 men enlisted and 8 died during the war.

RMS *Lusitania*

A controversial and important naval engagement took place on 7 May 1915. RMS *Lusitania*, a Cunard ocean liner, was identified and torpedoed by German U-boat *U-20* and sank in eighteen minutes. The vessel went down 11 miles off the Old Head of Kinsale, Ireland, killing 1,198 and leaving 761 survivors.

The *Lusitania* was sunk before very much was understood about evasive tactics when faced with submarines. The contemporary investigations both in the UK and the United States into the precise causes of the ship's loss were obstructed by the needs of wartime secrecy and a propaganda campaign to ensure that all blame fell upon Germany. Argument rages still as to whether the ship was a civilian or military target; at the time she was sunk, she was carrying a large quantity of rifle cartridges and non-explosive shell casings as well as civilian passengers. Diving is still being attempted to settle this argument once and for all.

Conkers for acetone

On the Western Front the troops had bullets but not the components for rapid fire. Conkers were used to help remedy the situation. On locations such as the Sandringham Estate, schoolchildren and other people were organized to collect conkers. Even the Queen reputedly helped. The conkers were taken to a munitions factory at Alexandra Dock where they were distilled to produce acetone which provided cordite. With this added to the firing mechanism, guns could fire more easily.

Zeppelins

Norwich prepared for 'air-raid action' sixty times during the war.

The first major warning was on 19 January 1915. Two Zeppelins were sighted at about 8 pm over Bacton, heading towards Norwich. The electricity supply for the whole city was turned off immediately. Zeppelins L3, L4 and L6, under the overall command of Zeppelin commander *Korvettenkapitän* Peter Strasser, took off from their base at Fuhlsbättel in Germany. L3 and L4 carried 30 hours of fuel, 8 bombs and 25 incendiary devices and were to attack military and industrial buildings on Humberside. L6, which carried Strasser, had to turn back as it developed engineering problems in the poor weather conditions. Weather also had a bearing on the two remaining airships which had to change their plans and eventually made landfall in Norfolk where L3 turned south-east towards Great Yarmouth and Zeppelin L4 flew north-west towards King's Lynn.

Zeppelin L3, under the command of *Kapitänleutnant* Hans Fritz, crossed the Norfolk coast between Happisburgh and Winterton and as it did so it dropped parachute flares to navigate its way from Martham towards Great Yarmouth. Bombs dropped on the town resulted in a crater 2 feet wide, a burst water main and the death of a large black dog.

Zeppelin L4 dropped incendiary bombs on Sheringham that caused a lot of damage but there were no fatalities. Thereafter it travelled to Brancaster Staithe, Hunstanton, Heacham, Snettisham and Sandringham, where much propaganda ensued as it could possibly be seen as an attack on the Royal Family although this is unlikely to have been the case. Much more likely is that the Zeppelins travelled wherever lights could be seen; unfortunate for King's Lynn which was

Zeppelin L3 that bombed Norfolk on 19 January 1915.

quite visible from the air. Here there were fatalities: Percy Goate aged 14 and Alice Gazely aged 26, both of whom are reported to have died from shock. After the raid L4 headed east and actually flew past Norwich, which was luckily shrouded in fog and had its lights out, and then was seen to pass Acle before flying out to sea to the north of Great Yarmouth.

There were various Zeppelin raids over neighbouring counties, notably Essex. Much is still not known of these sorties but it is assumed that often the machines were attempting to reach London. The *Eastern Daily Press* was scathing about the indiscriminate nature of these attacks and had this to say on 28 May:

> The second zeppelin raid on Southend was of the usual character; the promiscuous dropping of deadly missiles on a sleeping town of non-combatants, without any pretence at serving a military purpose or achieving anything upon the

forwarding of the war. On this occasion the German savages succeeded in killing two women and maiming a little girl; an accomplishment which the poets of the Fatherland will no doubt celebrate in fresh verse as they have already celebrated the *Lusitania* massacre.

Forage Corps

The Women's Forage Corps was established by the government in 1915; the British army at this time was chiefly reliant on horsepower and the demand for forage (horse food) was massive. The Forage Corps came under the auspices of the Army Service Corps (ASC), the unit responsible for keeping the British army supplied with all its provisions except weaponry and military equipment. Becoming the Royal Army Service Corps in 1918 in recognition of its huge achievements during the conflict, it was also known informally as 'Ally Sloper's Cavalry'. Ally Sloper was a character from a popular British comic strip of the time, all about a crafty rent-dodging schemer. The 'cavalry' bit may have been a sarcastic reference to the large numbers of work draught horses and mules that the ASC deployed in their work.

The work of the hospitals

Norwich in particular and Norfolk in general played a crucial role in caring for the sick during the war. Throughout the conflict the Norfolk War (General) Hospital at Thorpe was the central hospital of fifty auxiliary hospitals scattered throughout Norfolk containing over 1,000 beds. In total 44,651 men passed through it. It was officially closed on 15 April 1919.

The first convoy was received on 17 October 1914 and more than 8,000 sick and wounded members of the forces were cared for. Tents were erected in the grounds and the *Eastern Daily Press* paid for a new ward. HM Queen Alexandra, accompanied by Princess Victoria, visited the hospital on 12 October 1918. The fund for the maintenance of military beds totalled £23,565 for the whole war.

The County Asylum was converted into a war hospital on 1 April 1915. Lieutenant Colonel D.G. Thompson headed up a team largely consisting of mental hospital personnel. There were 2,450 beds.

There were also many smaller hospitals such as one called Sunnyhill that was originally situated in Larchwood, the home of the

Soman family in Thorpe, but in May 1915 moved to the larger Sunnyhill. One receiving belated recognition and currently being researched by the Brundall Local History Group is Brundall House, turned into an auxiliary war hospital from October 1914 to October 1916; the commandant was Margaret Harker of Blofield Hall.

In addition there were the following:

Norwich Palace Hospital: 40 beds; cases treated 224.
The Convent, Norwich: 14 beds; cases treated 361.
The Close, Norwich: 35 beds; cases treated 600.
Carrow: 32 beds; cases treated 341.
Catton: 28 beds; cases treated 668.
Thorpe, Connor: 23 beds; cases treated 608. Worked under the order of Saint John of Jerusalem.

The head of each establishment was called the commandant.

Harry Daniels VC

CSM Harry Daniels.

One of Norwich's most celebrated soldiers is Harry Daniels. At present a road is named after him in Wymondham, the town where he was born, but in 2015 a campaign was begun to erect a permanent memorial to him in his home city of Norwich.

Harry Daniels was born in 1884, the thirteenth child of a baker in Wymondham, Norfolk. He joined the army at a young age and served abroad in India.

He was 30 years old and a company sergeant major when he was awarded the VC. On 12 March 1915 at Neuve Chapelle, France, his unit – the 2nd Battalion of The Rifle Brigade (Prince Consort's Own) – advanced towards the German trenches across no man's land. The stretch ahead was blocked with barbed wire and under constant enemy fire. Daniels and another man, Cecil Reginald Noble, ran to the front to cut the wires. They were both wounded and Noble died later of his wounds. Their 1915 citation read: 'When their battalion was impeded in the advance to the attack by wire entanglements, and subjected to very severe machine gun fire, these two men voluntarily rushed in front and succeeded in cutting the wires.'

Daniels became a local hero in Norwich, and when he returned home crowds gathered to cheer and shake his hand. The sheriff presented him with a purse of gold to mark the grateful thanks of the city. He elected to stay in the army after the war and died in Leeds on 13 December 1953, his 69th birthday.

Rupert Brooke

The poet Rupert Brooke was staying at Cley on the Norfolk coast when he heard of the outbreak of war. Frances Cornford, granddaughter of Charles Darwin, was with him at the time and wrote:

> A young Apollo, golden-haired,
> Stands dreaming on the verge of strife,
> Magnificently unprepared
> For the long littleness of life.

He did not speak for a day until Frances Cornford asked: 'But Rupert, you won't have to fight?' to which he replied 'We shall all have to fight.'

W.B. Yeats called him 'the handsomest young man in England' and he had an illustrious group of friends. He joined the navy and, following his death from septicaemia in April 1915 when his unit was sailing to Gallipoli, Winston Churchill wrote that he 'was all that one would wish England's noblest sons to be in the days when no sacrifice but the most precious is acceptable'. He died on 23 April on board a hospital ship moored off the Greek island of Skyros and was buried in an olive

Rupert Brooke.

grove there later the same day as his unit was due to leave. Brooke passed away 'with the sun shining all round his cabin, and the cool sea-breeze blowing through the door,' according to his friend, William Denis Browne, who sat with him to the last.

Unlike his famous contemporaries Wilfred Owen and Siegfried

Sassoon, Rupert Brooke saw no fighting and he epitomized for many the youthful idealism and devotion to country felt during the first year of the war. In 1912 he had written *The Old Vicarage, Granchester* which ends with the famous words:

> ... oh! yet
> Stands the Church clock at ten to three?
> And is there honey still for tea?

His patriotic sonnet *The Soldier* was read from the pulpit of St Paul's Cathedral in April 1915. It opens with the much-quoted lines:

> If I should die, think only this of me;
> That there's some corner of a foreign field
> That is forever England.

Recently a bundle of papers has been opened by the British Library that details his love affair with the poet Phyllis Gardner.

There is a Rupert Brooke society based in Norwich at www. rupertbrooke.com

CHAPTER 4

1916: The Realization

1916 at a glance

• 1 January: Armoured car squadron raised in Cromer lands in Russia for service in support of Tsar's army.

• 24 January: Government announces conscription is to be introduced.

• 21 February: Battle of Verdun begins; it is to last ten months, with more than a million casualties.

• 25 April: Lowestoft bombarded by German navy.

• 29 April: Longest siege in British military history results in fall of Kut-al-Amara in Mesopotamia; the beginning of a horrific ordeal for hundreds of Norfolk soldiers.

• 31 May–1 June: Battle of Jutland; the allies endure heavier losses but the capability of the German fleet is permanently compromised.

• 5 June: Lord Kitchener among hundreds lost when HMS *Hampshire* hits mine off Orkney.

• 1 July: First day of the Battle of the Somme, the bloodiest in the history of the British army.

• 28/29 July: Claud Castleton, born in Lowestoft, earns posthumous VC.

• 28 November: Zeppelin destroyed off Lowestoft by aircraft flying out of Great Yarmouth's North Denes naval air base.

• 7 December: David Lloyd George becomes prime minister.

The young lads went, the young fathers, and then the middle-aged... Women and old men, schoolboys and soldiers worked in the fields...
Peace Souvenir, Jarrold and Sons, 1919.

Jarrold and Sons printing division

As previously mentioned, the famous Norwich firm of Jarrold and Sons owned – besides a department store and private library – a printing works. By 1916 stationery production was turned over almost entirely to war needs with millions of writing pads and compendiums being made for the troops. Christmas gifts were made for men at the front and included pocket wallets and leather goods, produced in their hundreds of thousands. A special department for the making of games and puzzles was also established and much appreciated by the hospitals and wounded men.

Many notable books were published including *The Blinded Soldiers and Sailors Gift Book*, *Told in the Huts* and *Shell Shocks*. *The Blinded Soldiers and Sailors Gift Book* is written from the point of view of a Special Constable patrolling the countryside. The night leads him to ponder on the men serving overseas who have lost their sight and the fear that must accompany their journey over the seas. He imagines them thinking about death and saying to themselves: 'I wonder if I shall ever see old England again?' Such books were enormously popular.

Numerous guides to the Home Country were made for Australian and New Zealand troops stationed here. In the latter part of the war, Jarrolds was engaged in making guides for the RAF. Some 165 men from the company signed up and 27 lost their lives.

The very sad case of the Browne family

James Browne was a gamekeeper from Hemblington, near Blofield who, after enlisting, was sent to Scotland, thus missing the birth of his fourth son, Harry. From Scotland, his unit was to be sent to France but, by lucky coincidence, was scheduled to call at Norwich to pick up more troops. He alerted his wife who set off on the 10-mile trip on foot with their four sons – aged 6, 4, 2 and a few months – to catch him briefly at the station. Stopping overnight in Sprowston, they reached the station only to find that the train had just pulled out.

Browne was never to see his family again, being killed at the

Somme. Much later, the *Eastern Daily Press* reported that Mr Browne's son Arthur had written an account of the family's 'narrow miss'. He concluded: 'Every time I think about this I have to cry.' The paper also reported that, on the village roll, James is listed wrongly as 'Brown'.

Norwich Volunteers: improvement needed

'We are always ready to undertake our neighbour's business, even to the neglect of our own.... There are two great military nuisances: the man who will do nothing and the man who insists on doing everything; the latter is the greater nuisance.' This opinion was expressed in a local paper regarding the difficulty of training volunteers, 14 January 1916.

On Boxing Day 1916 there was another sham fight for the Norwich Volunteers. A wagon was conveying stores, in this case hot coffee, to Swainsthorpe and had an option of roads. The Cyclist Company had to find the road used and mount an ambush. As there were far more cyclists than soldiers, a great many of them had to switch sides. The ambush was duly accomplished and everyone retired to Swainsthorpe and drank the coffee.

Subsequently, efforts were made to improve the military efficiency of the Volunteers. They were 'sworn in', had to have a certain physique and level of fitness and were drilled to an extent where many exhausted businessmen began to wonder if life might be easier in the regular army. By the end of the war there is no doubt that they had become a very efficient fighting force, but happily this never needed to be proven.

Sea defences strengthened

Enemy seaborne landings were seen as quite possible. In consequence a series of concrete pillboxes were built in a line from Weybourne to Sea Palling, with some following the seaward side of the River Ant. About two dozen remain today and can be seen at Bradfield, Weybourne, Stiffkey, Bacton, Stalham, North Walsham, Aylmerton, Thorpe Market, Beeston Regis and Great Yarmouth.

Zeppelin attacks commence in daylight

The Zeppelin alert of 31 January 1916 was at first disbelieved as the first Zeppelins were seen when it was still light, just before 5 pm. It was never thought that an attack would commence before dark. Yet two hours later, after the electricity had been switched off and the city was in complete darkness, an estimated thirty bombs were dropped that shook the houses below. It may have been because the Zeppelins chose to remain at a very high altitude that they all missed physical targets, although causing great disruption and damage to the county as a whole. The raid lasted over twelve hours and at one time, just before it ended, a Zeppelin was clearly heard, with its engines vibrating in the early-morning air, over Thorpe Station which offered no help to the bombers as it was in complete darkness.

Norwich Union Headquarters in Surrey Street, designed by George Skipper.

The most serious threat of the war occurred on Sunday, 1 October 1916. Zeppelins were reported 50 miles off the coast at 7 pm and by 8:05 pm one was immediately over Lowestoft. An hour later a third was reported over Stowmarket and a few minutes after this another approached Trimingham from the sea. The railway service at Thorpe was closed down and electricity to the city disconnected. At about 9:30 moving lights were seen near Costessey and the city reverberated to the sound of Zeppelin engines. At 9:40 four bombs were dropped around Cromer and by 10:18 two engines were clearly heard in the city, one approaching from the east and one from the west. Just after midnight a Zeppelin was 'heard' clearly over Magdalen Road Police Station and at about 3:15 four bombs were dropped, mercifully landing in Eaton Park, around 5 miles out. The Zeppelins then moved out to sea. It is estimated that ten in all were used by the enemy, four of which targeted Norwich specifically.

The local press was scathing about the supposed bombast of the German Zeppelin crews alongside their almost total lack of military

'Protection': a plaque inside Aviva.

success. Comic pieces were written depicting the 'heroes' returning to their families awash with Iron Crosses boasting of how they had sunk a destroyer, smashed Norwich to pulp and, just for fun, diverted to London where they blew up the Tower. It is certainly true that the German press on several occasions announced the destruction of Norwich Union's headquarters in Surrey Street where lookouts were stationed nightly to watch for Zeppelins. There was a similar situation regarding U-boats: although very successful in sinking shipping, they nevertheless regularly claimed the destruction of British ships that were, in fact, safely anchored in port.

Tanks

On June 4 the first two machines – nicknamed 'Little Willie' and 'Mother' – that were to have a decisive effect on the war arrived at a top secret military base on the Norfolk/Suffolk border for testing. Norwich engineers played a crucial part in the subsequent testing of these new-fangled and utterly frightening devices. Norwich was later to hold a very successful fund-raising campaign involving 'tank week' when these machines rattled and rolled past the old Guildhall into the market square. They were also perfect for standing on to make speeches, as the local dignitaries discovered. By 1918 450 tanks were to begin the final and decisive advance against the enemy.

Lucy Bignold – direct descendant of Thomas Bignold, the founder of Norwich Union (now Aviva) – speaking at Norwich Tank Bank Week, April 1918.

Tank Bank Week in the Market Place, Norwich.

The testing ground was chosen because the area was the most desolate part of the county, the land being bombed to make it more closely resemble the terrain of the Western Front. The location was so secret that it was guarded by large numbers of Volunteers.

Captured German gun and the Lord Mayor of Norwich, Sir G. Chamberlain.

Wartime organizations

Organizations for a great many purposes proliferated during the war.

One of the most vital was the City of Norwich Tribunal that dealt with claims for exemption from military service from 1916 to 1918. Chairman throughout was Dr E.E. Blyth and Major J.A. Berners was the military representative. The chairman was presented with a silver bowl at the last sitting on 22 November 1918. The tribunal held 154 meetings, the number of applications being 7,484, about 1,500 of which came up for consideration more than once. A total of 5,028 exemption certificates were issued; there were 790 appeals, of which 90 only were upheld.

The Norfolk Appeal Tribunal sat throughout the conflict. Men who objected on whatever grounds to active service were often asked to serve in a non-combatant role, such as in the medical or cooking sections. The following cases were reported in the *Norfolk Chronicle* of 21 April 1916. The tribunal sat at Shirehall, the Earl of Kimberley presiding:

Mr Walter Joseph appeared in support of the application of a Norwich pawnbroker and jeweller with several departments. Exemption was asked for a son, 19, who manages one of the departments.

The chairman said a youth of 19 could not manage such a business as that. Mr Joseph said that if Pitt could manage the Empire at 21, this young man could manage a pawnbroking business at 19. The tribunal decided that the youth must serve.

Norfolk Tribunal.

The case of a young Quaker was adjourned for a fortnight in order to give him time to join the Friends' Ambulance Unit.

An appellant from Reepham said he refused to take any part in the destruction of human life. Appeal was dismissed.

A Norwich clerk, single, 24, said he could not take human life. He was asked if he would resist a German advance. He said 'No'. Appeal dismissed.

The year 1916 was a very busy one for the Tribunal. On 9 June it considered the following cases:

• A baker, appealing for his son, 19, single, said he was indispensable to the business and that they supplied bread to the Yarmouth Isolation Hospital. Lord Kimberley replied what an extraordinary thing it was that everyone had a contract with this hospital and that they must eat a very large amount of bread (laughter). It was quite impossible that the tribunal should let off boys of 19 or 20. Refused.

• A Costessey coal merchant, 35, single, appealing for an extension of the time allowed by the local tribunal, said that he had been in business for ten years and had accrued debts and needed to dispose of things. Lord Kimberley asked which was the more important – men to fight in the war or the coal merchant's little business? Appeal was dismissed.

• On another occasion, on 14 July, a widow who operated two wherries appealed for her son, 19, who was the only man she had left, her other men having gone yachting and were not due to return until the autumn. Lord Kimberley remarked that she could not keep a boy of 19, and it was a disgrace that men should go and fiddle about in boats at this time. The boy was exempted only until 11 October. Final.

Norwich Police Court also continued to sit. The *Norfolk Chronicle* records the following in their edition of 20 September 1916:

Arthur Lake of 1 Tuns Yard, Oak Street, charged with stealing six boxes of Gold Flake cigarettes value £1 6s 8d. Prisoner pleaded guilty saying he was very sorry for what he did. Sentence: one month's hard labour.

The YMCA did much work for soldiers quartered in Norwich and Norfolk. By the last year of the war, the Association in St Giles Street (the building sadly being finally closed and sold in 2014) controlled some twenty-five centres around Norwich. The YMCA organized social and educational activities for an average of 20,000 soldiers who used St Andrew's Hall every week.

Some 115 War Savings Associations were formed under the chairmanship of Sir Eustace Gurney. These were formed as independent units in factories, business houses, railway stations, schools and churches. In war certificates, £686,000 was raised. One elementary school alone furnished over £3,000 and many subscribed £1,000 and £2,000. During Tank Week at Norwich £1,057,000 was raised and the Norwich people raised £1,500,000 towards a Victory Loan in 1918.

Many people deposited their money into the Post Office. One man who was not happy wrote to the *Norfolk Chronicle* on 28 February 1916:

Re War Savings
Sir, I asked my wife to start a book for me with 15s 6d. She came back with a message that I must go myself and be signed by me in the presence of a post office official. When I had the opportunity I did this, and then was told that every time 15s 6d was deposited I must go myself and go through the same performance.
    Am I likely to put more money in? I don't think!
    DISGUSTED of Cromer

The Voluntary War Work Association served in many ways. Here is a letter sent to the local press on 5 October 1916:

Sir, an urgent requisition has come to Norfolk and Norwich to supply 1500 pairs of mittens by Oct 15 for the use of British troops in Mesopotamia. We should, therefore, be most grateful for gifts in money or kind for this purpose.
Hon Sec Norfolk and Norwich Branch of the Voluntary War Work Association

The Norfolk Regiment Prisoners of War Help Committee was run throughout the war by Mrs Grissell and Miss F.W. Burton, the latter receiving an OBE for her work.

Coastal-class airship, Pulham St Mary.

The Pulham Pigs

Some 18 miles south of Norwich lies the village of Pulham St Mary. From 1916 this became the base for the airships known affectionately as the 'Pulham Pigs' that flew sorties out over the North Sea on the lookout for German submarines. By the end of the war, 3,000 men were based there.

After the war the base remained as the headquarters for the building of the gigantic R34 airship – 200 metres in length and 30 metres in height – that made the first east–west air crossing of the Atlantic in 1919.

By 1917 the base was also undertaking pioneering work into parachuting, becoming the headquarters of the Parachute Experimental Staff.

Food for the troops

Overheard in an Orchard:

> Said the apple to the plum: 'Well, anyway, old man, they can never ask us what we did in the Great War!'
> From celebrated war cartoonist, Captain Bruce Bairnsfather.
> (Tommies' rations invariably contained plum and apple jam and the appearance of any other variety was cause for celebration.)

Just the logistics of feeding the army were impressive: by the end of the war, the ration strength of the British army was 5,363,352 people worldwide, including 2,360,400 on the Western Front alone. To feed all these men, the Army Service Corps had expanded to a strength of 12,000 officers and 320,000 men, the size of the entire British army sent to the Continent at the outbreak of war.

The men might have occasionally missed a meal or got a bit bored, but the nutritional value of what they ate was very good. The calorific intake of an average soldier was much greater than that of a civilian. Soldiers ate an estimated 4,600 calories a day compared with a working man's 3,400 a day at home. The army diet was, however, particularly high in protein, leading to problems with boils and constipation. As a result, the amount of meat had to be reduced. All men received the same rations and the ranks were always fed before the officers, although horses were often given priority over both. Serving men were able to supplement army offerings with food sent from friends and family at home. They could also sometimes buy food at local cafés and homes.

Curry became more widely consumed during the war as its herbs and spices made the food more appetizing when eaten cold. The main staple in the trenches, however, was corned beef or bully beef: cooked and preserved tinned meat, chiefly from Argentina. The other tinned staple was 'Maconochie': a pork (or beef) and beans meal produced in Scotland. Many hated it and, in the dark humour of the trenches, referred to it as a 'war crime'. Vegetarians were given additional milk and sugar. Cooks were taught to make bacon go twice as far by dipping the rashers into flour or oatmeal, to prevent too much being lost with the rendering of the fat.

Some recipes from the front line
Where possible, of course, good fresh and tasty food could be provided by cooking it on the spot. As the war progressed the cooking was done ever closer to the front line, many cooks being killed as a result. Also, as the availability of ingredients could not be relied upon, it was often up to the cooks to do their best with whatever supplies were to hand and adapt times accordingly; therefore some of the following may seem a little vague! Here are a few sample recipes of the time:

Brown stew
Ingredients: meat, onions, flour, mixed vegetables, pepper, salt, stock.
Method: Take the meat off the bone, remove fat and cut into small pieces. Mix together flour, half an oz of pepper and half an oz of salt. Put stock in bottom of cooking vessel and dredge meat in flour. Add any onions and vegetables, cut up into cubes, to the meat and place in cooking vessel. Ensure stock only just covers ingredients and cook for 3 hours, stirring occasionally.

Potato pie
Ingredients: meat, potatoes, onions, pepper, salt, stock.
Wash and peel potatoes and cut into slices. Bone the meat, saving some fat. Mix in tin dish with onions or other vegetables. Add pieces of fat where meat is very lean. Add salt and stock to cover. Cook for 15 minutes to each lb of meat. Turn meat once during cooking.

Curried fish
Ingredients: fish, water, pepper, salt, curry powder.
Clean and cut fish into large chunks of about 4 oz. Poach until cooked. Keep the cooking water. Mix flour, pepper, salt and curry powder in a bowl with some of the liquid to form a paste. Add remaining liquid and heat until thickened. Pour over fish and serve.

Milky biscuit pudding
Ingredients: biscuits, milk, sugar, currants, mixed spice, candied peel.
Soften biscuits in cold water as necessary. Wash and chop currants. Add sugar and place in baking vessels. Add milk, spices and peel. Place over low heat and cook to taste.

(Tommies' biscuits were notoriously hard and the soaking part of this recipe could take several hours.)

There were also about 30,000 troops at home in Norfolk at any one time. They were supplied and canteens set up for them by Norwich grocers Copeman's.

CHAPTER 5

1917:
Seeing it Through

1917 at a glance
- 15 March: Tsar Nicholas II abdicates.
- 6 April: The United States enters the war.
- 19 April: Norfolk territorial units suffer their greatest loss in a single day during an attack on the Turkish-held city of Gaza.
- 17 June: Zeppelin L48 shot down over Theberton, north Suffolk.
- 16 July: T.E. Lawrence and Arabs liberate Aqaba in Jordan.
- 31 July: Third Battle of Ypres – or Passchendaele – begins. By November the allied line had advanced 5 miles at a cost of half a million casualties, of which 140,000 were fatal.
- 7 November: The British take Gaza.
- 11 December: The British liberate Jerusalem.

Two soldiers in a trench. One says to the other: 'Of course, I should not be here at all. I am not a poet.'

City life
Norwich continued to take its entertainments. The local press carried details of the many shows being put on around the city, including one at the Hippodrome. This featured a variety programme and was playing to packed houses. The Four Swifts topped the bill, an act involving juggling and clubs. There was also a Pierrot Troupe and songs by Miss

Lillian Carter, one of which – *My Hero* – went down particularly well. There was a mime act, the Five Flying Barnards and Brandon and Brand, who sang songs, danced and joked.

Norwich received a visit from Mr Austen Chamberlain in March. The *Norwich Mercury* reported:

> The first word of the stirring speech delivered at St Andrew's Hall, Norwich, on Tuesday evening, when Mr Austen Chamberlain, Secretary for India and a brilliant son of an illustrious father, spoke on National Service was 'I'. The last was 'Duty'. Both were spoken by the Lord Mayor of the City, and together they made by no means a bad motto for use in regard to National Service. They have been the watchwords of the old city through the many storms and centuries of national history, and they are its watchwords today.

Boots the Chemist reported that it operated 587 shops throughout the country and 'The number of men enlisted AVERAGES OVER FOUR FROM EACH BRANCH' (original capital letters).

The *Eastern Daily Press* of 2 July 1917 reported on the Dedication Window to Edith Cavell in the parish church of Swardeston:

> Since her noble death everything associated with her life has acquired a world-wide interest and requests received by the family and vicar of Swardeston for information have revealed some extra-ordinary forms of hero-worship. One person lately wrote asking for exact particulars of the design, dimensions etc of the vicarage in order that he might build a similar house for himself.

It was also reported on the same day 'that our Norwich VC (Harry Daniels) has just been promoted Captain'.

Eight days later the paper had the sad news that Second Lieutenant Orville Dwight Haist, 23, Canadian, had been killed at an East Anglian aerodrome: 'He attempted to rise from the ground before flying speed had been obtained with the result that he "stalled" the machine. One wing fell and the machine nose-dived to the ground. The officer died in hospital.' Such tragic events were commonplace in these early days of flying.

It was, however, on the same day also able to write of 'A GREAT EXPLOIT':

TO ESSEN AND BACK
The bombarding of the Krupp factory town at Essen by Sergeant-Aviator Maxime Gallois on Friday night was more than a gallant exploit by an airman, it was a reminder to the Germans that their cities are no more immune from air attack than ours. Gallois' machine was one of 84... and it is worthy of note that this powerful fleet of bombing aircraft was assembled, carried out its mission, and returned to its starting point with the exception of only 2 machines in sixty-six hours.

The courts continued to be busy. At Norwich Shirehall, Charles Banham of Hellesdon, refuse collector, was summonsed for stealing 81lb of crystallized sugar, 42lb rice, 79lb tea, 54lb ham, 16lb peas and 8lb tapioca to a total value of £17.16s, the property of the Army Canteen Committee. He was committed for trial. On 31 August Rose

Troops in the Market Place.

Snelling of 36 Bell Road was summonsed for a breach of the lighting regulations at 9:25 pm on 23 August. The Chief Constable stated that since the summons was served he had found that the defendant's husband had been killed in action. She was a woman in poor circumstances and had ten children. The Bench inflicted a fine of 1s. A week later saw Lucy Lincoln, widow, of 15 Ninham's Court summonsed by Elizabeth Tyrrell, neighbour: 'Complainant stated that last Wednesday morning defendant said she was dirty and smacked her face.' The Bench found the defendant guilty and fined her 2s 6d.

Harry Cator VC, the soldier from Drayton

Harry Cator, a railway worker's son, was born in 1894 and educated at Drayton School. He was married to his childhood sweetheart from Great Yarmouth on 2 September 1914 and signed up the next day.

On 9 April 1917 he was part of an attack on the German lines near the French town of Arras. The British advanced but were suffering heavy casualties from a German machine-gun unit. With the hard-won gains under threat, Cator and another soldier, under heavy fire themselves and in full view of the enemy, advanced across open ground towards the machine gun. His comrade was killed but Harry Cator made the machine-gun post and silenced the gunners. He continued to hold the post allowing the British to advance, taking 100 prisoners and capturing five machine guns.

Sergeant Harry Cator.

He later recalled how he had dashed to within about 50 yards of the German trench. He then dropped down in an attempt to trick the enemy into thinking he was dead. He wriggled to the edge of the parapet:

> I just peeped up, and as luck would have it, they were not looking my way but were busy cutting the men down who were trying to advance on their right. There were five in all, one working the gun and the others feeding ammunition. It was the work of a moment! My revolver spat five times in quick succession, and the Germans went down…

A few days later a shell shattered his jaw and he was still recovering in Bristol Hospital when he heard he had won both the Victoria Cross and the French Croix de Guerre.

Harry had already won the Military Cross in summer 1915 for helping rescue thirty-six men stuck in no man's land. He refused a commission on that occasion but accepted promotion to sergeant.

After the war he worked for the Post Office and the Unemployment Assistance Board. He and his wife settled in Sprowston where he died in 1966. He lies in Sprowston Cemetery.

Sidney James Day VC

Sidney was born in Lakenham, Norwich and attended St Mark's School. He was the second Norwich man – Harry Daniels being the first – to win the VC.

The youngest of a family of nine brothers and sisters, he was born in the 1890s at St Anne's Lane, off King Street. His father had worked at Morgan's Brewery before running a lodging house on Ber Street that became the famous Jolly Butchers.

When war was declared he joined the Suffolks. In the summer of 1915, by then a lance corporal, he went to France with his battalion just in time for the Battle of Loos. During one battle he found he was the only soldier in his platoon who was not injured. He

Corporal Sidney Day.

picked up his wounded officer, Lieutenant Stevens, and was carrying him away from the battlefield when the officer was shot and killed by a sniper. Then some months later during the Battle of Mons Sidney was shot twice but managed to crawl 3 miles to a dressing station and was returned to Norwich and Wymondham for treatment.

By early 1917 he was back in France and it was during bitter fighting around Ypres and Passchendaele that his actions earned him the Victoria Cross. He was in command of a bombing section detailed to clear a maze of enemy-held trenches. He did, killing two machine-gunners and taking four prisoners. He then went on alone and seized a trench bomb, throwing it away from other soldiers, where it exploded.

(Left) Sidney James Day VC after a reception in his honour in Norwich.

(Below) Wounded soldiers from the front lines are taken off trains at Thorpe Station.

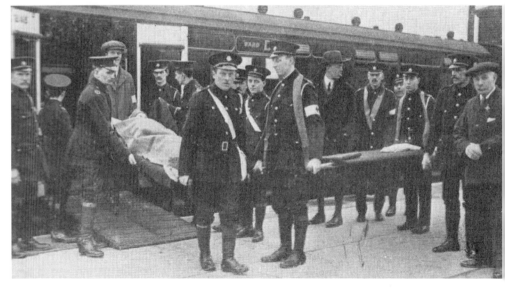

His actions saved many lives. He then cleared the trench and remained in an advanced position for sixty-six hours during which time he came under intense hostile shell and rifle grenade fire. His actions were described as 'an inspiration to all'.

When he finally made it back to Norwich he was a hero. Everybody wanted to shake his hand. Crowds gathered to cheer him. He returned to his old school and a party was thrown in his honour at the Mission Hall in Trafalgar Street.

Sidney went back to France where he was then captured and held as a prisoner until the end of the war.

Back in civilian life he worked for the Electric Light Company in Norwich before moving to Portsmouth where he worked in the dockyard and ran a shop. He died in 1959, aged 68.

The Mann brothers

In November 1917 the *Eastern Daily Press* carried the moving tale of the four Mann brothers from Norfolk. William aged 23, Oscar aged 31 and Percy aged 21 had all been killed within a short while of each other in 1916/17. To save the family further heartbreak the authorities sent the remaining brother Alfred, serving in the Black Watch, home to Norfolk where he saw out the war.

The Victoria Cross

The Victoria Cross is the highest British military decoration, awarded for valour 'in the face of the enemy'. It was created in January 1856, during the reign of Queen Victoria, to recognize courage shown in the Crimean War. The medal features a bronze cross bearing the crown of St Edward surmounted by a lion and is inscribed 'For Valour'. The VC has been awarded 1,357 times, with 628 being won during the First World War. Of those, 159 were gained posthumously. The largest number awarded in a single day was nine on 1 July 1916, the first day of the Battle of the Somme. On that day the British army lost 19,240 men. For the Royal Navy the largest action of the war came in 1916 at Jutland where four VCs were given. Nineteen were awarded to the Royal Flying Corps. Among Commonwealth troops who won the medal were 71 Canadians, 13 members of the Indian army, 63 Australians and 11 New Zealanders.

So great were the losses in some parts of the forces that black humour seemed the most appropriate response. The Machine Gun Corps, for example, was known as 'the Suicide Club'.

Local soldier Percy Thrower

Norwich has many cherished memorials to 'ordinary' soldiers in the numerous churches throughout the city. One such is in St George's, Colegate in Coslany, previously mentioned as one of the areas where unlicensed pubs proliferated to the despair of magistrates. The memorial tablet to those of the parish who gave their lives in the Great War is situated just inside the door of the nave and records thirty-five names. Below this are photographs of Edward Florance, Edward Tooke and Leonard Pert. Another from this parish, Percy Edward Thrower, lived at 19 Calvert Street, the son of Alfred and Rebecca. Percy was a carter for a corn merchant. He joined the 7th Battalion Norfolk Regiment and died of wounds on 3 August 1917 aged 24. He is buried in the British Cemetery at Monchy-le-Preux.

A daring rescue

On 6 January 1917 a Swedish steamship *Fernebo* was passing off the Norfolk coast, laden with timber en route to Gävle on Sweden's east coast, when it ran into a German mine and split in two.

Shortly before this, the Cromer lifeboat *Louisa Heartwell* with famous coxswain Henry Blogg at the helm had already been at sea for several hours, rescuing sixteen people from a stricken Greek steamer, the *Pyrin*. However, with the Sheringham and Sea Palling lifeboats unable to launch, the crew put to sea again, in conditions so severe that they were unable to clear the beach.

Meanwhile, six of the *Fernebo*'s crew launched a small boat that capsized. They were rescued by people on the beach. In the late afternoon the *Fernebo*'s two halves had grounded, half a mile apart. The *Louisa Heartwell* tried another launch at 9:30 pm. They lost three oars with another five smashed, but the crew eventually managed to get alongside the wrecks and rescued the crew of eleven. Applause from locals greeted the boat as it came home at 1 am on 10 January.

Mr Blogg received an RNLI Gold Medal, acting second coxswain William Davies was awarded the Silver Medal and twelve of the crew were awarded the Bronze Medal. The *Fernebo* wreck was removed from Cromer beach in 1922.

The Hoggett family: five lost

The Hoggett family was spread around the villlages of Little and Great Cressingham, Hilborough and Threxton and lost five members during the war. Sapper Albert George Hoggett was a member of the Royal Engineers and died on 9 August 1916, being buried at Mametz in France. Herbert James Hoggett signed up immediately on the declaration of war and was killed in France on 28 April 1917, aged 20.

Two cousins, James and Albert, were killed when the troopship *Royal Edward* was torpedoed off the coast of Gallipoli on 13 August 1917. Rifleman William Hoggett lost his life on 16 August 1917, aged 20. A brass tablet in their memory was placed in the church of St Andrew, Little Cressingham by Herbert's mother Emily and is still there.

The church server from Hoe
The loss of a church server prompted his home village to commission a set of candlesticks in his memory. Two candlesticks bearing the name of Corporal Thomas Parker were found stowed away in a corner of a church vestry in St Andrew's Church early in 2014, as reported in the *Eastern Daily Press*. The inscription read: 'In memory of Corporal T.A. Parker DCM, killed Passchendaele 1917. Server.' He was aged 21. Thomas is wrongly commemorated on Dereham's roll of honour rather than Hoe's, and also on the Arras Memorial in France.

Three brothers
Three brothers from the south Norfolk village of Harleston – Frederick, John and Stanley Borrett – were killed within seven months of each other, two in Palestine and one in France in 1917.

The extraordinary story of Norwich Components
Some of the firms that made an invaluable contribution to the war effort have already been mentioned. Perhaps no story, however, is more dramatic or important than the story of Norwich Components.

On 10 September 1917 the *Eastern Daily Press* ran the following story:

> GREAT FIRE IN NORWICH
> A MIDNIGHT BLAZE
> A few minutes before midnight on Sunday the fore hooter at the works of Norwich Components Ltd, near Foundry Bridge, brayed forth and then minutes later the compact but commodious building of five stories was a blazing cauldron... A fuse on the second floor is supposed to have started the fire.

In just a few years Norwich Components produced more than 2 million fuses for shells, and paid out more than £150,000 in wages to the 250 men and 970 women who worked at the factory during its brief but quite extraordinary existence.

It also operated a social committee and according to one of the men behind the company, William ffiske of Boulton & Paul: 'Hockey, tennis, dancing and musical entertainments were indulged in, and the best of feeling existed between the Board and their employees.'

The firm came about when the East Anglian Munitions Committee appealed to all shell-makers to consider the question of making fuses. Boulton & Paul regretted that they couldn't respond as the company was already making an immense variety of munitions of war and had run out of space at Riverside. They were also making aircraft. However, William ffiske realized the importance of fuse-making, so he and Mr H.P. Gould registered Norwich Components Ltd. It was established at Foundry Bridge Mills, then occupied by Colmans.

It was initially hoped that the firm could make up to 4,000 fuses a week. However, when they joined forces with Messrs Laurence, Scott & Co. Ltd, that estimate went up to 10,000 a week. Incredibly, as things turned out their output, inspired by an American engineer of genius, Mr R. Neil Williams, was worked up to 36,000 fuses a week. The company experimented with making the fuses from cast-iron, not brass, and when they succeeded the saving to the country was enormous.

Then disaster struck and it was only due to the hard work of the Norwich Fire Brigade that the fire was restricted to the factory itself. Immediately a new factory was established at the Old Skating Rink (which is still there, although now an oriental warehouse).

Upon declaration of the Armistice the factory was ordered to close and this remarkable story ended. As the enterprise was solely a product of war needs, the story has been comparatively forgotten until recently but now renewed research is being undertaken.

The House of Barnards

This is another firm that deserves a very honourable mention and that increased their efficiency and production as the war progressed.

Founded in 1826, the invention of wire netting by Mr Charles Barnard in 1884 transformed the business. During the war every machine was working at full pressure and in 1915, 1916 and 1917 some 6,994 miles of netting was produced. It was used in trenches, for bomb shields and for transport over desert sands.

Chapelfield Gardens just before the start of the war. The magnificent iron pavilion was built as an exhibition piece by Barnards. Subsequently the council bought it for £500. Although now gone, part of the original ironwork has been preserved and can be seen as a gate and fencing in the corner of the park that faces Chapelfield Shopping Centre.

In addition the company made hundreds of yards of special hand-woven wire for the war in the Balkans; large heating stoves for the American army in France; wire screens for high-explosive factories; and cooking ranges.

Some 200 employees enlisted, 15 being killed including the managing director's son, Mr Charles F. Bower, who died just upon being promoted to captain. The company encouraged its staff to buy war bonds by offering interest-free loans and £1,650 was raised in this way.

Food for the people of Norwich
From a postcard series 'Romance 1917', a man is saying to his sweetheart: 'Darling, every potato that I have is yours.'

When the Great War broke out in 1914 Britain was heavily reliant on food imports, particularly from Canada and America, two-thirds of her food being produced abroad. Therefore keeping the shipping lanes open in the Atlantic and North Sea became vital. Germany was determined to starve Britain into submission and consequently sent many submarines to sink supply ships operating along these routes. Between 31 May and 1 June 1916, one of the greatest sea battles in naval history took place, the Battle of Jutland. A vital campaign was fought to ensure that the people of Britain continued to be fed.

At one point two years into the war, Britain found herself with only six weeks' worth of wheat and on the verge of starvation. Rationing was both regional and voluntary at first. Sugar had been rationed in some places from 1916 and other products, especially potatoes, were in short supply from 1917. General voluntary rationing was tried from February 1917 but was not really effective. At the end of 1917 compulsory food rationing began regionally and by February 1918 it was countrywide. By April the main foodstuffs including meat, butter and cheese were all rationed. Some products such as cheese and butter continued to be rationed after the war.

On 1 January 1917 the *Norwich Mercury* reported that a Food Production League for Norwich had been established with the following objectives: a) to increase the production of home-grown food; b) to encourage the growing of vegetables; c) to give expert advice; d) to help with seeds, manure etc.; e) to get volunteer labour; f) to encourage the keeping of poultry and other animals; g) to organize collection of waste; h) to arrange for distribution of surplus crops; and i) to organize collection and distribution of seedlings.

Alongside the report was an article: 'How to succeed with an allotment'. Norwich people have always been keen growers of food and even today there is a long waiting list for the considerable number of allotments on the city outskirts.

Recipes featuring Norfolk food

The following are a few recipes recommended at the time. It is not surprising that emphasis was placed on produce for which Norfolk and its coast were famous, such as fish, sugar beet, potatoes, carrots and apples.

Fish cakes

Take the remains of cold fish, a few mashed potatoes, a little chopped parsley, a few breadcrumbs, pepper and salt and anchovy sauce. Work these together until no lumps remain; make into a flat cake and fry until nicely browned. Make a sauce with a little fat, salt, a squeeze of lemon, and a wineglassful of stock thickened with flour; pour this over the fish cake, and serve very hot.

Fish custard

Take any cold fish, remove all bones and skin, lay it in small pieces in the bottom of a pie dish, and mix with a little salt and pepper. Mix a dessertspoon of flour smooth in a teacupful of milk; add one beaten egg and a piece of fat about as big as a walnut, creamed but not oiled. Pour it over the fish, and bake for half an hour or so in a moderate oven.

Kedgeree

Boil two tablespoons of rice, add any fish previously cooked; it should be well picked from the bone in shreds; beat up an egg and stir it in just before serving, but don't let boil after egg is added. Serve with egg sauce.

To increase or augment butter

Wash four ounces of butter or margarine in cold water; drain, and work into butter half a teaspoonful of salt. Then add four ounces of cooked sieved potatoes, still warm but not hot, and go on beating till they are thoroughly incorporated with the butter. Leave it in a cool place, and when cold, shape into pats.

Fish sausages

Take two cupfuls of cooked fish, two tablespoonfuls of cooked rice, some dried herbs, one small egg and salt and pepper. Mix all together and form into sausages. Roll in flour and cook in hot fat.

Sugar-beet syrup

Peel and scrape the sugar beets; when you have got them absolutely clean, cut them up into thin strips, place in a pan with enough water to cover them, and boil for two hours; then simmer for eight hours. Then strain off the juice, and bottle, and cork it closely.

Chop up the drained strips very small and dry them in a moderate oven. They are said to be useable in puddings instead of raisins, but will need soaking.

Calves feet, boiled

Take two calves feet, the rind of a lemon, mace, cloves, mignonette and pepper to taste.

Boil till bones drop out. Then place the pieces of meat on the dish it is to be served in. Boil liquor till it clarifies, and reduce to just sufficient to serve each piece. Last of all sprinkle with chopped parsley. Sufficient for four persons.

Recipes were given for herrings: baked, boiled, broiled, marinated and potted.

Herrings and Potatoes

Wash and boil some potatoes in their skins, carefully, so that they do not break or get too soft. Drain them, peel, and slice them rather thickly. Keep them hot. Fry lightly a chopped onion in one ounce of fat. Dust in some flour, add three tablespoons of vinegar, salt and pepper, and a bay leaf, and not quite a pint of water. Put the pan to simmer. Take two red herrings, wash them well, cut them lengthways, and remove the bones. Cut up the flesh small, and let it simmer in the sauce for a few minutes. Put in the potatoes next, stirring carefully so as not to break them. Then add two ounces of fat and one gill of milk, and stir all well over the fire till it reaches boiling point.

Carrot soup

Take three pints of stock, and add the following: one onion finely minced and four carrots grated, fried in one ounce of fat; one ounce of rice, one teaspoonful of maize flour; herbs and parsley to taste; bacon rind and scraps. Boil up, and add salt and pepper to taste, let simmer one and a half hours; put through a sieve, reheat and serve.

Apple and Ginger Jam

Well wipe, peel, core and slice, four pounds of cooking apples. Place in preserving pan with one teacupful of water, the grated rind and juice of two lemons, and a quarter of a teaspoonful of ground ginger. Cook till nearly a pulp; then add one pound of glucose and two pounds of Demerara sugar; boil up again until the jam will set; put into pots and cover whilst hot.

Trench Pudding

Have two tablespoons of rice boiled in half a pint of milk and water, until the liquid is absorbed and the rice tender. Mix in two ounces of shredded cocoa butter (or suet) and one dried egg, with a few chopped dates or a little sugar, and steam them in a greased basin.

Sugar-Beet Pudding

Take six ounces of sugar beet, wash well and peel, place in boiling water sufficient to cover, let simmer for two hours. Remove from water, chop small, and place in a covered casserole with a very little water, and let cook until soft enough to pulp through a sieve.

Add to the sieved beet the following, well mixed: two ounces of cooked sieved potatoes, four ounces of G.R. flour and a quarter of a breakfast cupful of fat; with a pinch of salt and the grated rind and juice of half a lemon. Last of all, moisten one teaspoonful of carbonate of soda and add. Blend thoroughly, place in a greased basin, and steam three hours.

Potato and Apple Pudding

Boil and mash one and a half pounds of sour apples; boil three potatoes, and add them through the masher to the apples; mix well, add four ounces of sugar, a cupful of water, and the grated rind of one lemon; one or two eggs can be added but these are not necessary. Beat well, place in a greased basin or mould, and steam for an hour and a half.

Gravy without Meat

Allow four large onions sliced to two quarts of water, a bundle of sweet herbs, a burnt crust of bread, two ounces of fat, some pepper and salt. When boiling, strain it, and add to it a tablespoonful of ketchup.

Haybox cookery

It was also recommended that households make something called a haybox. This was a box with hinges and a lid with secure clasp to the front; alternatively a tin with lid. Inside are several thicknesses of newspaper, 4 inches of hay, and all is covered in flannel. Food is initially cooked on a stove and transferred to the haybox for long, slow cooking. For example, potatoes are cooked for five minutes on the stove, then one and a half hours in the haybox; boiled rice is cooked for two or three minutes on the stove and then two and a half hours in the haybox; coarse oatmeal porridge is boiled for five minutes and then left in the haybox all night, resulting in a perfect, cheap and nutritious breakfast.

Prisoner-of-war camps set up in Burnham

The seven settlements of Burnham had a very busy last two years of the war, as from the summer of 1917 thousands of German prisoners captured by the British on the Western Front were sent there, primarily to Burnham Norton.

The local press strikes a new note

As the year ended, the tone of the press changed. Increased confidence of victory was in the air. On 13 September the *Eastern Daily Press* carried the headlines 'WESTERN FRONT – BRITISH AIR SUPERIORITY' and 'SPLENDID EXPLOITS', along with reports of 'SWEDISH DUPLICITY'. On 21 September it reported: 'The news from Flanders has been eagerly awaited for some days past, and splendid news it is now that it has come... Our men have swept over the whole of these positions' (Glencorse Wood, Inverness Copse and the area round about the Ypres-Menin Road). 'Yesterday was a day of unqualified victory.' The next day it ran the headlines:

THE HARASSED HUN
HOW WE ATTACKED ON THURSDAY
FEAT ON A GERMAN PARAPET
ENEMY'S SHATTERED DIVISIONS
THE BROKEN DEFENSIVE
REAL MEANING OF THE VICTORY
COUNTER ATTACKS ALL COSTLY FAILURES
DISMAYED PRISONERS

Three days later saw a total dismissal of any 'discussions': 'We should be mad to dream of any such discussion of terms, of any letting loose in the world again of a wild beast government... of which we have at last got the whip hand.' It then went on to satirize the Kaiser: 'He is going to bring peace to the world by "battering in with an iron fist and shining sword" upon his enemies who still dare oppose him. He has "in the Lord of Creation above an unconditional and avowed Ally on whom Germany can absolutely rely".' Such promises of German victory were, the paper declared, 'absolute bunkum'.

Almost as if to emphasize that normal life may soon be returning, the *Eastern Daily Press* also found time to praise Norfolk's favourite literary son's latest novel: 'SIR RIDER HAGGARD'S LATEST – "Finished" 5s. Needless to say Sir Henry, as ever, excels in his wizardries... We envy those who come to this book for a first reading.'

CHAPTER 6

1918: The Final Blows

1918 at a glance

• 3 March: Treaty of Brest-Litovsk heralds peace between Soviet Russia and Germany.

• 21 March: Germans launch Spring Offensive along a 50-mile front.

• 25 March: Arthur Cross from Shipdham, Norfolk awarded VC for action during the German Spring Offensive; later adds a Military Medal.

• 30 March: Billingford-born Gordon Flowerdew earns a posthumous VC in one of the final cavalry charges in history.

• 5 April: British and Australian troops hold the line and halt the German Spring Offensive outside Amiens. Second, third and fourth German offensives follow.

• 22 April: Allies carry out raids on Ostend and Zeebrugge.

• 15 July: Second Battle of the Marne; Germans now on the defensive.

• 8 August: Second Battle of Amiens starts. A decisive allied victory bringing a return to a more mobile form of warfare as trenches are breached; the opening phase of the Hundred Days' Offensive that ultimately leads to the end of the war.

• 27 September: British Offensive on the Cambrai Front leads to the storming of the Hindenburg Line.

• 29 September: Norwich-born Ernest Seaman, rejected for front-line service earlier in the war, is awarded a posthumous VC during the British advance near Ypres.

• 3 November: Austria-Hungary signs an Armistice.
• 8 November: Peace negotiations begin between the allies and Germany.
• 9 November: Kaiser Wilhelm II abdicates; revolution breaks out in Berlin.
• 11 November: The Armistice is signed at 5 am and comes into effect at 11 am. Three minutes before then, Canadian Private George Lawrence Price is killed while on patrol, the last to die on the Western Front.

Unchanging love

When the war is over, mother dear,
When the war is over, mother dear,
When the bands all play and the people cheer,
As the boys come marching thro' the dear home town,
Joy-bells ringing gaily as the sun goes down;
Tho' your heart is aching, mother dear,
For your soldier boy never fear,
I'll come back some day, and kiss your tears away,
When the war is over, mother dear.
(Popular printed postcard of 1918)

Who can forget the day of Armistice…? That sunny morning the multitude thronged at a word to the heart of Norwich and filled it with their shoutings and their songs. A bloom of flags innumerable broke in all the streets, on all the towers. St Peter's epic peal sent the message out in stirring changes, and in the crowd there were those of pensive face who could find no speech, who hardly could listen to the bells with dry eyes.
Peace Souvenir, Jarrold and Sons, 1919.

How the local press reported the year

Much was naturally made of the bravery of the troops. The New Year's Honours *Gazette* reported that twelve men had been awarded the Distinguished Conduct Medal and fifteen the Meritorious Service Medal. On 7 January the *Norwich Mercury* reported the Food Ministry saying 'we have got to tighten our belts and be prepared for appreciably reduced meat rations'. In the same edition was the wonderful news: 'Today 632 repatriated men were landed at Boston, Lincs on their return from... German internment camps – 370 civilians, 235 soldiers and 27 officers.'

Dire news was given of the state of affairs in Germany. On 9 January the *Evening News* reported on 'the Hun Way of suppressing criticism' during 'stormy scenes at Fatherland meeting' which entailed 'CRIPPLED SOLDIERS BEATEN WITH STICKS' (original capital letters). On 8 November it reported:

> Peace is imminent, and official messages from Berlin suggest that Germany is anxious to have it at almost any price... There are apprehensions in Germany of a coup d'état... The German Press is prepared for the worst. The *Lokalanzeiger* says that the consequences of the demand for peace may be catastrophic.

The Harvest Festival of this year was a particularly joyous affair, as described by the *Norwich Mercury*:

> Harvest Festival at St Peter Mancroft
> Never before perhaps has harvest given such cause for thankfulness as in these days. And it was evidently with this thought in mind that hundreds of busy people turned out and... in a service of praise and thanksgiving... No such impressive harvest thanksgiving, brief as it was, had surely ever previously taken place within its walls.

The courts, as ever, were kept busy. One unusual dismissal of appeal was reported in January: 'Norwich, before Mr William Carr Ethel Cracknell appealed her 14-day sentence that on 17 Sept 1917 she did harbour Victor Duncan, a deserter from H M Army. Appeal dismissed.'

Meanwhile, city life was beginning to return to normal. The *Evening News* offered H. Samuel watches at 17s 6d; Norwich Hippodrome – now gone – was showing the pantomime *Aladdin and the wonderful lamp in Seven Scenes and Pleasing Dresses* twice nightly at 7 and 9 pm; 100 business cards cost 4s 6d; a new tractor could be had for £250; a shipment had been obtained of 'New Furs and Pelts'; Fieldings had a new consignment of gramophones; Nimrod's would cure your asthma; and Curl Bros – now Debenhams – had some 'Dainty New Blouses'. The *Norwich Mercury* advertised a newly-crafted inlaid mahogany bureau for £2 17 11d and a cosy fireside chair for 25/11d;

and girls who grew listless were advised to take 'Dr Williams' pink pills for pale people'.

In one important respect the local press of the time was sombre in tone: inevitably, there were many stories of soldiers lost or missing. Often the entry was a few sentences only, headed 'Norwich Lance-Corporal reported missing' or 'Death of Private Kendle'. However, one of the more detailed stories reported on 2 January concerned Jack Long, one of six serving soldier sons of Mr George Long, coxswain of the Institution lifeboat, who had been killed on 30 November. His professional life was briefly told. He originally enrolled in the Coldstream Guards where his training – shooting fowl on the mud marshes of Blakeney – had given him an excellent eye and an accuracy of aim that made his shooting prowess a vital asset to the British war effort. There were many letters, too, from worried parents asking anybody at all who may have knowledge of the whereabouts of their missing son or husband to contact them.

St Peter Mancroft Church: the bells of this famous church have announced major victories over the centuries including the defeat of the Spanish Armada, Lord Nelson's victory at Trafalgar in 1805, the Duke of Wellington's defeat of Napoleon in 1815 and Armistice Day 1918.

Food shortages

In early January, with food becoming very scarce, the Ministry of Food announced 'Lord Rhonda's Rationing Model' which was a scheme for preventing queues in shops. It was voluntary for the immediate future and the main provisions were:

- Every customer should be registered with one shop for the purchase of a particular foodstuff and not allowed to buy it elsewhere.
- The shopkeeper should be required to divide his weekly supplies in fair proportion amongst all the customers registered with him.
- No shopkeeper should be allowed to register more customers than he can conveniently serve.
- The scheme should initially apply only to butter, margarine and tea until such time as further experience had been gained.

In 1918 the government issued the *Win-The-War Cookery Book*.

Food hoarding was also a big problem and on 13 March 1918 the following appeal was made in *The National Food Journal*:

The Government is endeavouring to see that every person has a fair share of food and it is therefore of the greatest importance that every member of the public should assist in maintaining a fair distribution of supplies. They should do this by refraining from buying more than their usual quantities of foodstuffs. Retailers should co-operate in securing a fair distribution of their stocks. Bakers generally are holding satisfactory stocks of flour and coal. The Executive Committee, appointed by the London Division Exchange, unanimously agreed that all market prices established on Friday last for all kinds of butter, cheese, bacon, ham, and lard shall remain the maximum prices until further notice. In some parts of the provinces there seems to be an inclination to put up prices, partly caused by a certain amount of panic buying, which, however, is being checked by traders and Co-operative Societies themselves. Some fish has been sent to London from Lowestoft by sea.

Women's Branch of the Board of Agriculture

In January 1917, the newly-created Women's Branch of the Board of Agriculture had been formed under the directorship of Meriel Talbot. Then in March 1917 a civilian women's labour force known as the Women's Land Army (WLA) was established. Healthy women over the age of 18 were eligible to join and after four weeks of training would initially receive a weekly wage of eighteen shillings. By 1918, 300,000 women were working as Land Girls, as they were known. The WLA played a vital role in helping Britain to increase her food production and become less reliant on imports.

The changing role of women

When Thetford's town crier John Clarke went off to war, his role was filled by his daughter Florrie, aged just 15. Her father survived and resumed his job once the war ended.

There were 7,123 women serving in the British Expeditionary Force in France in 1918. This figure must be considered alongside the total number of people in the Imperial forces, some 3.22 million.

Independently of the war, the women's suffragette movement was reaching a peak at the beginning of the conflict with many protests including the alleged burning down of Britannia Pier at Great Yarmouth in April 1914. As mentioned earlier, the suffragettes were not prepared to let their campaign run out of steam just because the country was at war and many people were shocked by the burnings, bombings and general destruction of property and artwork that continued.

The biggest stimulus to female employment, however, was the mass signing-up of husbands, sons and brothers. Before the war, women principally worked in domestic service and production. Now they found themselves moving into traditional 'male' jobs, although often at a lower rate of pay than the people they replaced. The reasons given for this were ingenious but mainly based on physical differences between men and women: size of hands, strength, and so on.

Boulton & Paul led the way in this respect: soon 1,226 women were employed and such was the degree of satisfaction of the Ministry of Munitions that they sent women out all over the country to show how things should be done. Women also helped to make boots for the army in several major Norwich firms as well as uniforms at Harmer's.

Accurate employment figures are impossible because many women simply took over the men's work on an informal basis, but as far as factories were concerned, in 1914 roughly 23 per cent of women were in employment and by 1918 that had almost doubled to 45 per cent.

However, not everyone was happy with this state of affairs. It was said by some that to broaden a woman's mind was somehow to limit her charm, some even using words like 'unnatural' and 'cruel' to describe the process. Behind all this, of course, were great anxieties: fear that the world was changing for ever, that the flower of the nation's youth was being annihilated, and now the fear that women were becoming independent, opinionated and had money to spend as they wished.

Where would it all end? The immediate answer to this question was the 1918 Representation of the People Act that gave the vote to 8.5 million women, while the Sex Disqualification (Removal) Act of 1919 made it illegal to exclude women from jobs purely on the grounds of their gender.

Cavell Memorial Home and the Specials

A proud day of celebration for the city in general and for the Specials in particular was when HM Queen Alexandra (Queen Mother), accompanied by Princess Victoria, came to the city on 12 October

Memorial to Edith Cavell in its new position alongside the Erpingham Gate to the Anglican Cathedral.

1918. She opened the Cavell Memorial Home and unveiled a statue of the nurse. Order was kept solely by the Specials, thus releasing the regular force for other duties and saving the city an estimated £300.

In June 1918 Mr Winsor Bishop and Mr E.E. Hines were awarded the Most Excellent Order of the British Empire. Every man in the Specials was given a silver star after two years' service, to be worn on the right sleeve of the summer tunic. Following Queen Alexandra's visit, they were presented with a blue enamel star inscribed 'A.R. 1918'.

The Lads' Club, sponsored by the Chief Constable – at this time Mr J.H. Dain – was helped by the Specials. A football match between the Specials and regular police that took place at the Newmarket Road Ground raised £126 5s 0d, mainly donated to the Lads' Club.

Bringing Edith Cavell home

After the war, Edith Cavell was brought back from Brussels to England. Exhumed on 17 March 1919, her body was found to be well-preserved and the features still recognizable. On 13 May it was taken to the station, escorted by British troops on the initiative of a certain Major B.L. Montgomery (later Viscount Montgomery of Alamein), then to Ostend and from there was taken by HMS *Rowena* to Dover. A special railway carriage bore the coffin to London on 15 May accompanied by members of the Cavell family, and a horse-drawn gun carriage took it through streets lined with spectators to Westminster Abbey, where the funeral service was attended by George V. Her family was offered the option of burying her at the Abbey but chose to have her return to Norwich.

The grave of Edith Cavell in Life's Green, alongside the Anglican Cathedral.

She was transported to Liverpool Street Station and then by train to Norwich, where the coffin was placed on another gun carriage and escorted to the cathedral by soldiers of the Norfolk Regiment for burial.

The funeral of Edith Cavell.

Queen Alexandra unveils the memorial to Edith Cavell in 1918. The Home for District Nurses named after her is behind on the right; it is now part of the Maids Head Hotel. The monument itself has been moved a few yards and now stands in front of the Erpingham Gate to the Anglican Cathedral.

The service was conducted by the Bishop of Norfolk.

London also has a statue of Edith Cavell by Sir George Frampton near Trafalgar Square and a Cavell Street in Whitechapel. In France and Belgium, Edith became a popular name for girls born after her execution, among them Edith Piaf.

Gordon Flowerdew VC and Sir Alfred Munnings: a double Norfolk and Norwich connection

Lieutenant Gordon Flowerdew.

Gordon Muriel Flowerdew was born in Billingford, Norfolk in 1885 and educated at Framlingham College in Suffolk. He later emigrated to British Columbia, where he took up ranching.

When war broke out in August 1914 he enlisted as a private in Lord Strathcona's Horse, and in January 1918 Flowerdew was given command of C Squadron of the same cavalry unit.

In late March, as the Germans approached Moreuil, Flowerdew ordered a cavalry charge. Although casualties were enormous, the charge so unnerved the Germans that they were never able to capture Moreuil Wood and their advance turned into a retreat in early April. This is often referred to as 'the Last Great Cavalry Charge', for which he was awarded the Victoria Cross. Gordon Flowerdew himself was mortally wounded during the charge.

It was Alfred Munnings, at the time a largely unknown war artist, who subsequently created the famous oil painting depicting this event.

Alfred was born in Mendham, Suffolk and at 14 began working for a Norwich printer. Despite losing the sight of his right eye in an accident in 1898, he pursued his dream of

Baron Manfred von Richthofen, the 'Red Baron', who remarked that he lost his lust for hunting for about fifteen minutes after he had shot down an Englishman. He was killed on 21 April 1918 following combat with a Sopwith Camel.

A Sopwith 1½ Strutter.

becoming an artist and in 1899 twice exhibited at the Royal Academy. He was elected president of the Royal Academy of Art in 1944 and knighted the same year. He died in Dedham, Essex on 17 July 1959.

Arthur Henry Cross VC

Arthur Cross was born in Shipdham, Norfolk. He was with the 40th Battalion Machine Gun Corps when he won his VC on 25 March 1918 for capturing prisoners and causing heavy casualties. He single-handedly approached and captured seven armed men, causing them to throw down their guns and take them and their tripods to British lines. His citation said: 'It is impossible to speak too highly of the extreme gallantry and dash displayed by this NCO...'

Lance Corporal Arthur Cross.

Arthur survived the war and died in 1965.

Ernest Seaman VC

Ernest Seaman was born in Derby Street, Heigham, Norwich in 1893. He was awarded a posthumous Victoria Cross for bravery just six weeks before the Armistice. On 29 September 1918 at Terhand,

Belgium he single-handedly captured two machine guns in one operation along with twelve prisoners, and then another on the same day, before being killed immediately afterwards. His citation said that 'his courage and dash were beyond all praise', and it was thanks to him that his company could push forward to its objectives.

Ernest was 25 years old and a lance corporal in the 2nd Battalion, The Royal Inniskilling Fusiliers.

Major Egbert Cadbury DSC, DFC

Many men who flew were killed even before seeing battle, such was the fragility of aircraft of these times. One who did not and lived until 1967 was Major Egbert Cadbury, a member of the legendary chocolate dynasty. He shot down a Zeppelin off the coast at Wells-next-the-Sea on 5 August 1918 and was awarded both the DSC and DFC.

Two Christmas cards for 1917 and 1918 sent home by the author's great-uncle Arthur. Arthur survived the war but succumbed to Spanish flu in 1919 in Mesopotamia where he is buried.

Norwich High School for Boys

The principal of the school, Mr J.G. Chapman, wrote in the Annual Report for 1918 that of the school's old boys who signed up he

> had been able to trace 350 of them who enlisted. Of these 150 hold commissions, but there are doubtless many others who have escaped my notice. Five have won the Military Cross; one the Military Cross and Bar; six, the Military Medal, one, the Distinguished Conduct Medal; one, the Distinguished Service Cross; one, the Distinguished Service Order, while six have been mentioned in dispatches.

Four masters and fifty-four 'boys' died.

The school paid for a miniature rifle range at a cost of £300. This was used daily by all regiments stationed in Norwich, including the Scottish and Bedfordshire regiments. It also formed a cadet corps which in 1917 and 1918 won awards and medals, making it the most efficient corps in Norfolk.

In 1918 the annual sports day raised £67 10s 0d, all donated to the Red Cross and the War Hospital of the Little Sisters.

Thankful villages

A 'thankful village' is one to which all soldiers returned safely after the war. One such is St Michael, South Elmham: a tiny settlement near Bungay where not one inhabitant was lost in the war. Eleven men – a fifth of the population – had enlisted.

It is one of only fourteen 'doubly thankful villages' in the country, where no one was lost in the Second World War either.

The Royal Family, Zeppelins and the mysterious disappearance of the Sandringham Company

Queen Alexandra witnessed a Zeppelin over Sandringham in September 1916. The household heard a noise at 10 pm and looked outside to see, in the Queen's words, 'this awful monster'. The house immediately put out all lights and the machine passed over but, after an anxious few hours, witnessed the return of the Zeppelin at 4 am. It dropped its bombs at nearby Dodshill, which received a royal visit the next day.

Armistice Day.

By 1916 the king, aware of food shortages, pledged that his entire household would give up alcohol for the duration of hostilities, rationed their own food and ripped up flower beds for vegetable-growing.

In 1908 100 men of the Sandringham estate had, at the request of King Edward VII, formed a Territorial Army unit. The 'Sandringham Company' was subsequently sent to Gallipoli where it mysteriously 'vanished' in 1915. In 1918 a mass grave of 180 bodies was found near to where it had disappeared. Debate continues to this day as to what exactly had happened to the company.

CHAPTER 7

Aftermath

The Fine City's loss

Norwich men served, and died, in many regiments all around the world.
The loss of life at Ypres and the Somme was unprecedented and
heartbreaking. The city lost 3,500 men in Flanders and Picardy and
other theatres of war. As previously mentioned, for some groups of
citizens, such as the Police Pals' units and the Sandringham Company,
the losses were inexplicably cruel. The crowded wards of Norwich
suffered too: 171 from the Parish of St Barnabas, Heigham; 119 from
St Bartholomew, Heigham; 92 from Eaton; 141 from Holy Trinity; 133
from St James; and 148 from St Mark, Lakenham.

*Presentation of medals in the Market Place, Norwich in 1919 by Major
General Sir J.E. Capper KCB.*

(Top) Memorial to the dead of both world wars above the Market Place with the castle in the background. It was originally in front of the Guildhall. (Below) A sideways view showing the fifteenth-century Guildhall – built between 1407 and 1413 – to the left.

Housing and recreation

Those who survived returned to a city little changed from the one they had left, beautiful certainly but with crowded living conditions and poor sanitation. New housing estates came into being and attempts were made to do something about the infamous Norwich Yards and other areas of poor housing. It took two decades, however, to basically eradicate them and redevelop the area to a good standard.

As the importance of health and recreation became politically significant, a fine set of public parks came into being, and the City Hall was built with a Fire Station and Weights and Measures Office nearby. Some people, notably the Norwich Society (formed in 1923), although accepting the need for change, were concerned that much of value could be lost and vigilance was always going to be needed to protect the glories of the old city. The Norwich Society is still very active today. Changes there have certainly been – the factory sites of both Colman's and Boulton & Paul now comprise riverside flats and the area that housed Caley's chocolate, mineral water and Christmas cracker production lines is a now a state-of-the-art shopping mall – but the city still has the same street plans in the central part as it did in Edwardian times. It is recognizably the same city.

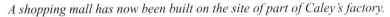

A shopping mall has now been built on the site of part of Caley's factory.

Chapel of the Royal Norfolk Regiment in the Anglican Cathedral, the Cathedral Church of the Holy and Undivided Trinity.

Floor stone in the chapel of the Royal Norfolk Regiment, Anglican Cathedral.

Nearly 12,000 lives! Such is the sheaf which Norfolk gave to swell the harvest of the war. It is a well-eared sheaf, the richest, by proportion, it would seem, in our whole English field. For the United Kingdom the number of killed or missing is one out of every 57 souls; in Norfolk it is one out of every 42. Also to this total must be added all the crippled; all the sick and, what is sometimes worse, all the wrecked in mind…

We cannot understand; we can only bow our heads and go to shape for them memorials in stone or brass…

Nor from any single rank or class did these go out to fight and fall with the stubbornness of our Viking stock, but from every class. All have drunk of the cup and shared the sacrifice as all have earned its glory.

Introduction to Norfolk Roll of Honour 1914–18 by Sir H. Rider Haggard, KBE

The Norfolk Cemetery

The Norfolk Cemetery in Bécordel-Bécourt in northern France has a special link to Norwich and Norfolk as it was formed by the 1st Norfolk Battalion and men from other units are also buried there. Private George Chase of the 1st Norfolks, originally from the village of Ruston some 17.5 miles north-east of Norwich, was the first man to be buried there. He was killed just two days after arriving on the Somme. The first of the 8th Norfolks to be buried there was Private Henry Digby of the 178th Royal Engineers who enlisted in Norwich and died on 15 September 1915. His was a tunnelling unit. William Arthur Cook from Grove Road, Norwich, previously employed by the *Eastern Daily Press* and attached to the Norwich Business Men's Company of 8th Norfolks, also lies there. He had represented England at football. He was killed on 23 November 1915, aged 30.

Memorial in the cloisters of Norwich Cathedral to the 34th Norfolk Divisional Royal Engineers.

New work for those who died

After the war a stained-glass window was created in Norwich Cathedral to commemorate the sacrifices made by Norwich soldiers. Below it is a brass plaque on which are the names of those who died. The Royal Norfolk Regiment has its own beautiful chapel in the cathedral.

Bradwell is planning a new memorial to the sixteen men who died, previously commemorated on a plaque in the church. It will cost £4,000 and it is planned that the local Boy Scouts will plant flowers around the border.

A fund of £100,000 has been announced to boost the restoration of the UK graves of our First World War VC heroes. The project aims to restore all those graves in need of repair including the Sprowston grave

Memorial window in Norwich Cathedral to the Norwich and Norfolk soldiers of the Great War.

Memorial in Norwich Cathedral to the men of the King's Own Royal Regiment, Norfolk Yeomanry, the 12th (Yeomanry) Battalion, Norfolk Regiment, and the 65th (Norfolk Yeomanry) Anti-tank Regiment RA who fell in both world wars. The names on the plaques are of those who died in the Great War. Those who fell in the Second World War are written in the Book of Remembrance.

of Norfolk's Harry Cator, as well as the Hampshire and London graves of Norwich man Sidney James Day and Shipdham-born Arthur Cross.

The *Eastern Daily Press* announced in 2014 that it was launching an interactive database for all the region's war dead. It aims to make this as comprehensive as possible in times to come. Anyone can check the details of their family members at www.edp24.co.uk/first-world-war-memorial

Memorial to those who fell in the Great War on the external wall of St Peter Mancroft.

The Worldwide Context

The Great War was a truly global conflict. This book clearly concentrates on Norwich, Norfolk and the United Kingdom but few parts of the world escaped the fighting completely.

Africa
A series of clashes saw German colonies taken over. Many were wary of the British after the recent Boer War.

Australia and New Zealand
The war is credited with forging a new stronger sense of national identity for both Australia and New Zealand as their troops fought in many arenas.

The Balkans
In many ways the epicentre of the war and the scene of much of its fighting, as the conflict swallowed up all the powers in the area.

Canada
When Britain declared war on Germany it did so on behalf of the Empire, bringing in Canada and the independent colony of Newfoundland. Some 619,000 men enlisted in the Canadian Expeditionary Force.

China
There was an attempt by the Japanese, aided by the British, to take the German colony of Tsingtao in 1914.

Eastern Front
Perhaps as many as 2 million Russians died in the almost 1,000-mile-long front from the Baltic to the Black Sea. The regime in Russia became fatally weakened.

Gallipoli
An amphibious landing in Turkey that was an unsuccessful attempt by Britain to strike a lethal blow on the Ottoman Empire.

India
By the end of the war 1,105,000 Indian personnel had been sent overseas. Indian troops earned eleven VCs.

Italy
Italy and Austria-Hungary fought a long and bloody war along their border.

Mesopotamia
A campaign fought in difficult conditions between Ottoman and allied forces for control of areas – now mostly in Iraq – containing oil fields vital to the British war effort.

Palestine
Another campaign fought between Britain and the Ottoman Empire.

USA
The United States entered the war in 1917 in support of the allies. Several events led the US to intervene, notably the sinking of the liner *Lusitania* by a German submarine as there were many American passengers on board.

Major Naval Battles
1. Heligoland Bight, August 1914: First naval clash of war; British victory.

2. Coronel, November 1914: German victory.

3. Cocos, November 1914: Australian cruiser HMAS *Sydney* forces German warship SMS *Emden* to run aground.

4. Falkland Islands, December 1914: British victory.

5. Dogger Bank, January 1915: British and German squadrons clash in the North Sea; indecisive, although victory claimed by the British.

6. Jutland, May 31–June 1 1916: Largest naval clash of the war; considered a British victory.

A City Centre Great War Walk

Norwich is a compact city and the following can make a rewarding walk at any time of year. As it is in the very heart of the city, a break or coffee can be taken at any time and the walk can be undertaken at a pace to suit.

Tombland – Edith Cavell statue. Go through the Erpingham Gate to:

Anglican Cathedral – stained-glass First World War window and chapel of Royal Norfolks. **Edith Cavell's Grave**. Retrace steps to Tombland and turn left. Follow road around and up to the right to:

Boer War Memorial. Continue round the Castle base and turn left, up sloping entrance or lift to:

Castle Museum. Wonderful collection of Great War memorabilia, letters, medals and artefacts. Leave Castle and

Boer War Memorial by G.E. Wade.

follow road past the Bell Hotel and turn left into Surrey Street. On the left is George Skipper's masterpiece:

Aviva HQ Surrey Street. Return to St Stephen's Street, turn left and cross road, entering:

Chapelfield Shopping Centre, site of Caley's. Leave by first floor exit and cross road to:

Forum and Millennium Library – many books, **Colman**'s library. Leave Forum and turn left, passing by the 1938 Town Hall by architects Holloway and Pierce. Cross road and stand in front of:

Market Square, War Memorial to both world wars. Carry straight on and cross over road to fifteenth-century Guildhall. Go inside to: **Caley's café** where Caley's chocolate is on sale. Leave café and proceed down gentle slope. In front is:

Norwich Crest on War Memorial.

Breath *by Paul de Monchaux which was commissioned by Norwich City Council in 2010. 'The Living Honour the Dead, Only a Breath Divides Them.' It stands immediately behind the War Memorial.*

Jarrold's store. Leave store and continue up Gentleman's Walk. Turn left into George Skipper's

Royal Arcade, built by George Skipper and looking almost exactly as it did in Edwardian times.

Time
A good half-day, or longer if you linger in maybe the Cathedral Church of the Holy and Undivided Trinity, Jarrold's, the Castle Museum, etc.

Distance
Maybe 3 miles, depending on how much you wander off course. It is easy to detour as the route has many interesting side streets and features. Walking conditions – flat or gently sloping.

Index